TEACHING

Emotional

INTELLIGENCE

MAKING INFORMED CHOICES

Adina Bloom Lewkowicz

SkyLight
Professional
Development

Arlington Heights, Illinois

Teaching Emotional Intelligence: Making Informed Choices

Published by SkyLight Professional Development
2626 S. Clearbrook Dr., Arlington Heights, IL 60005
800-348-4474 or 847-290-6600
Fax 847-290-6609
info@skylightedu.com
http://www.skylightedu.com

Senior Vice President, Product Development: Robin Fogarty
Director, Product Development: Ela Aktay
Acquisitions Editor: Jean Ward
Editor: Dara Lee Howard
Project Coordinator: Sue Schumer
Cover Designer and Illustrator: David Stockman
Book Designer: Bruce Leckie
Production Supervisor: Bob Crump
Production Assistant: Christina Georgi
Proofreader: Catherine Shapiro
Indexer: Candice Cummins Sunseri

LCCCN 98-61534
ISBN 1-57517-127-9

2330V
Item Number 1702

Z Y X W V U T S R Q P O N M L K J I H G F E D C
06 05 04 03 02 01 00   15 14 13 12 11 10 9 8 7 6 5 4

DEDICATION

To my parents, Zeev and Corinne Bloom, who respected my ability to choose and taught me to do so wisely.

CONTENTS

PREFACE

The poignant words of an eighteen-year-old boy inspired the writing of this book. In my second year of graduate school in social work, my field placement was with an agency that served chemically dependent adolescents. On the final day of my internship, an eighteen-year-old boy came up to me and said, "Adina, I'm so happy that I became addicted and that I'm now in recovery because I came out so much better a person!"

I was rendered speechless, dumbstruck by the riveting thought that what he received through the recovery process could have been his birthright! The knowledge and skills with which to develop positive, healthy, successful children and prevent future problems are available and teachable!

Armed with the words of that eighteen-year-old boy, a fervent belief in the potential of each individual to be fully actualized, a background in education, psychology, theater, and social work, and an unbridled desire to save the world, I chose to write this book. Teaching youngsters to make informed, effective choices regarding their emotional, physical, mental, and social well-being can lead to the development of happy, healthy, high-functioning adults. As more and more adults feel good about themselves, manage their emotions effectively, communicate clearly, learn how to resolve conflicts, and meet their needs in positive ways, we can move as a society toward the development of a healthy, high-functioning civilization. At the very least, we will end up with healthier, higher-functioning classrooms and happier students and teachers!

I would like to thank those educators who share my vision and will attempt to bring it to fruition, one child at a time. I would also like to thank SkyLight for the opportunity to try to leave the world a better place than I found it. In particular, I would like to thank Jean Ward, who was the first to share my vision, Sue Schumer, and Dara Lee Howard, who edited the manuscript.

I thank my children, Ellis and Zanna, for putting up with all the hours devoid of "Eensy, Weensy Spider." I thank my husband for all the hours he had to sing "The Wheels on the Bus," for all the years of supporting me while I wrote this book, and for all the hugs and reassurances throughout the process. I give thanks to my mother for being my secretary/wife, nanny/friend. I thank my mentors, Zeev Bloom, Ken Simpson, Howard Goldstein, and Mitchell Fields, for their inspiration. And I thank an eighteen-year-old boy for giving me the final impetus to write *Teaching Emotional Intelligence: Making Informed Choices*.

INTRODUCTION

A TEACHER'S LAMENT

I have just about had it up to here! One more argument or fit of tears and I think I will scream. I know that I am supposed to be a super teacher with an endless supply of patience and energy, a technique for every situation, and a solution for every problem, but sometimes I cannot believe that he just crumpled up his assignment again because it was not exactly the way he wanted it to be. Oh terrific. There she goes, grabbing his pencil yet one more time. I can see the headlines now: "Youth who stole pencils in her formative years arrested for grand theft!"

I want these children to grow to be happy, successful adults. I do everything I can. I talk with them and reason with them, but sometimes it is as if I were talking to the air. The same things keep happening over and over again.

With youngsters as they are, it's difficult enough to get all the subjects covered that must be taught. Now you want me to teach something else? How can I find the time? Why should I bother?

WHY TEACH EMOTIONAL INTELLIGENCE COMPETENCIES?

It is evident that young people are engaging in many harmful behaviors leading to increasingly damaging results for themselves and for society. Alcohol and drug abuse are increasingly widespread and appear among younger and younger age groups. The teenage pregnancy rate grows each year. Since the 1980s the level of childhood stress and depression has been steadily rising along with the number of juvenile crimes, runaways, and suicides (Gibson 1989).

Classrooms are filled with youngsters displaying a wide range of concerns and behavioral problems that teachers have little time and few techniques to address. Students suffer from poor self-awareness, low concentration, lack of motivation, little self-discipline, low self-esteem, poor communication, an inability to express feelings effectively, difficulty in resolving conflicts, and a significant amount of emotional pain.

Anxious, unhappy, angry youngsters do not make ideal students. As they try to focus their attention on getting their needs met and feeling better, little concentration is left for learning. As they search for and find inappropriate outlets for their emotions, they misbehave. Encouraging a classroom full of such students to learn and behave effectively can be very time consuming and frustrating.

Teachers can help lessen their students' frustrations, make classroom time more productive, and prevent behavioral and learning problems by providing their students with a body of information and a set of skills with which to make informed, positive, and independent choices regarding their emotional, social, physical, and mental well-being (Dewhurst 1991; Meyer 1990). This book provides teachers with the tools to do just that.

WHAT IS TEACHING EMOTIONAL INTELLIGENCE?

Teaching emotional intelligence capabilities is not a pipe dream. Nor is this book a program of gimmicks and catchphrases. It is a curriculum that is based on the understanding that students think and behave ineffectively because they lack the skills and information with which to make more effective cognitive and behavioral choices. This curriculum provides teachers with the tools to transmit those important skills and that vital body of information.

Goleman, in his groundbreaking research on emotional intelligence (1995), spoke to the great need for developing mastery over the emotional realm so that one can make healthy, positive choices. He discussed the importance of providing the opportunity for each person to develop positive emotional habits as well as basic human competencies. He categorized these competencies into five domains: self-awareness, managing emotions, self-control, empathy, and handling relationships. Goleman's research indicated that these emotional and social competencies are learnable and cited the school environment as an ideal context within which to develop them.

Goleman's research further indicated that in order to truly develop these competencies, one must teach youngsters the skills to challenge their often inflexible thoughts. He spoke to the importance of checking one's thoughts against available evidence, thus offering cognitive guidance before the emotional switch goes into effect, triggering ineffective choices.

This book is centered around just this process. Students are taught that every thought, feeling, and behavior is based on a choice that has been made. Often, however, these choices are made by default, out of habit, or based on faulty or no information. The curriculum helps the teacher help students make choices con-

SkyLight Training and Publishing Inc.

sciously and effectively. The lessons in this book help students become aware of their feelings, how their feelings are expressed, and how their feelings influence their choices. They help students examine the beliefs and thoughts that trigger their emotions. Students are taught to examine their beliefs and thoughts for errors in logic and to change assumptions to provable beliefs (Ellis 1990). They apply this process across myriad situations, learning how to stop, think, and choose well.

HOW TO USE THIS BOOK

Teaching Emotional Intelligence is designed for anyone who works with young people and has the context within which to develop emotional intelligence and informed choice-making skills. *Teaching Emotional Intelligence,* which can be used by kindergarten through high school teachers, is also appropriate for use by guidance counselors, day care providers, club leaders, program directors, camp directors, and parents.

Teaching Emotional Intelligence falls most directly within the curricular areas of health, social studies, and language arts. However, Reflective Detective activities extend the lessons into the areas of math, science, and history. These activities can be expanded to address more fully these curricular areas, and additional activities can be developed to extend the lessons into other areas of the school curriculum. As an aid, each lesson begins with a listing of the curricular areas addressed as well as the emotional domains and multiple intelligences covered.

The first four chapters of the book provide the background about emotional intelligence and informed choice making necessary to use the rest of the program. Use the rest of the book in the order most beneficial to your situation. If a lesson does not fully address your needs in a particular area, expand the lesson as necessary in order to address specific issues in greater depth.

Using the activities in this book, students can be encouraged to develop the emotinal competencies as described by Goleman. They will increase their self-awareness, learn how to better manage their emotions, build self-control, grow in empathy, and develop their ability to handle relationships effectively. They will have the opportunity to use positive choice making in their daily lives, which is the goal of a mental health curriculum (Gibson, 1989; Meyer, 1990). Students will build emotional intelligence by learning how to make choices consciously and effectively.

WHAT METHODS ARE COVERED?

A number of approaches—skill development, multiple intelligences, and drama— are used extensively throughout the book.

SKILL DEVELOPMENT

In order to execute increasingly effective life choices rather than merely understanding how to make them, youngsters must develop a range of life skills or human competencies as described by Goleman. In his book, *Emotional Intelligence*, Goleman (1995) cited a number of highly effective emotional education programs. A common thread in each of these programs is a focus on developing these life skills.

Throughout the course of this book, there are opportunities to expose students to a comprehensive repertoire of life skills fundamental to making increasingly effective life choices, including relaxation, cooperation, effective use of body and voice, emotional awareness, effective expression of feelings, clear communication, assertiveness, conflict management, and goal setting (Cowan and Clover 1991; Deline 1991; Erin, Dignan, and Brown 1991; Jones, Kline, Habkirk, and Saler 1990; Rolan 1991; Rotheram 1982).

MULTIPLE INTELLIGENCES

In his definitive work, *Frames of Mind*, Gardner (1983) described the multiple intelligences that each person possesses. These include verbal/linguistic, musical/rhythmic, logical/mathematic, visual/spatial, bodily/kinesthetic, naturalist, interpersonal, and intrapersonal. Gardner speaks of the great need to develop each of these intelligences, thus developing each individual to his or her fullest.

In this book, each of the intelligences is addressed and a range of learning styles is covered. Much of the content of the curriculum focuses on the intrapersonal and interpersonal intelligences. Through the use of this approach, students become more self-aware and personally and interpersonally effective.

In addition, this approach affords students the opportunity to become involved physically, intellectually, and emotionally. Chapman (1993) suggested a number of methods for enhancing the development of intelligences, some of which are used in this book: discussion; reading; writing and lecture; focusing on verbal/linguistic, naturalist, and logical/mathematical intelligences; movement and dramatic techniques; developing bodily/kinesthetic and musical/rhythmic intelligences; and art activities that enhance the visual/spatial intelligence.

DRAMA

This book provides a wide range of active experiences in the choice-making process. The information and skills addressed in the curriculum are presented in such a way that youngsters learn the material by application. In this way, the material can be truly used rather than merely understood.

Drama is used as a primary medium with which to observe and evaluate choices and rehearse alternate options. The active, immediate, and personal exploration that drama demands is a highly effective method to teach choice-making skills in a way in which students may truly learn and use them (Mayer 1990).

Many lessons in the book use a dramatization focused on the concept being explored. An aspect of the concept is chosen, and a story is developed and acted out in the form of a brief scene. The scene then is discussed, and the choices made in the scene are evaluated. Then, new choices are made and a new story is developed and enacted, reflecting those choices.

The thought of using drama may seem daunting, as it conjures up images of talented actors and actresses performing great works of theater on a stage. This could not be further from the truth in its use in this book. Neither talent nor previous experience are necessary.

The basic skills of dramatization are developed and used not to produce a high-quality play but rather to fully experience and examine the concepts in the curriculum. Skills are built through a progression of exercises presented in the early lessons of the curriculum. These exercises concentrate on developing the full range of use of body and voice to express thoughts and feelings and on developing the ability to create thoughts and dialogue appropriate for a specific character in a specific situation.

The use of drama calls for participation at the physical, verbal, emotional, and intellectual levels. Therefore, using drama to explore a variety of concepts necessitates a more complete involvement in that exploration than simply discussing the concept. As students involve themselves in the dramatization process, they are less able to remove themselves from the concept being explored than they might be if they were exploring the concept through discussion alone.

Using drama as a mirror with which to observe one's own as well as others' responses affords students the opportunity to become aware of nuances of the concepts explored in ways not possible using other methods. Dramatization allows for the exploration of a concept in a manner that most closely resembles real life. This makes it easier to apply the learning to real life situations, using drama as an opportunity to first rehearse skills and choices, and then apply them in one's own life.

HOW IS THE BOOK ARRANGED?

Following the introduction, the book is divided into three parts. Each part addresses one of three major life proficiencies: feeling positive, thinking wisely, and acting sensibly. Each chapter deals specifically with one of Goleman's emotional competencies by presenting lessons that consist of activities that support understanding and development of the competence through personal experience with and practice of techniques and methods. At the end of the book are a blacklines section, which contains the handouts for use with a class; an appendix, which provides summary activities that supplement the chapters; references; and an index.

LESSONS

Each lesson begins with an introduction that outlines the salient points of the emotional competence being addressed. This is followed by a list of the targeted intelligences and pertinent curricular areas. The heart of a lesson is the activities, which are designed to progress step by step toward the competence of interest. The activities may be used as written, may be changed to meet your needs, or you may develop your own. At the end of a lesson, modifications for some of the activities for two different grade levels are suggested. These modifications consist of hints for adapting subject matter or presentation to better fit primary grade children or middle and high school students.

ACTIVITIES

Some suggested activities necessitate that students behave in ways that are un-usual in some classroom settings. For example, some activities require that students move around rather than sit in chairs. Other activities, such as brainstorming, may lead to overlapping conversations rather than each student speaking in turn.

Although these activities may necessitate a certain flexibility in the classroom, they do not lack structure. Each activity is designed with a specific outlined framework to maximize its effectiveness. As a result, these techniques provide students with a high level of involvement in the topics explored.

Although some of the techniques require some flexibility, they can be adapted to your level of comfort. For example, you may feel more comfortable trying some of the more physical activities with a smaller portion of the class. Or, if you are concerned about the noise level in the classroom, you may want to structure an activity such as brainstorming so that students raise their hands before they speak.

There are several features in the activities that recur and are presented in a standard manner. These features are the use of handouts, the use of the detective metaphor, and the use of dramatic scenes.

HANDOUTS In most activities, one or more handouts for students are provided. These handouts are collected in the blacklines section near the end of the book. You are welcome to photocopy and use them for instructional purposes in your classroom.

One section that recurs in many of these handouts is the Inquiry section. This section is an opportunity for each student to openly express feelings, opinions, and experiences; to explore a certain topic and develop material for further exploration; and, if shared with another, to find out that other classmates may have similar experiences and feelings. An inquiry is presented in the form of an unfinished sentence that students complete, based on the first thing that comes to mind. There are no right or wrong answers. If the student shares this personal response during a class discussion, no one comments on it, and the handouts are not to be evaluated.

A number of the handouts are variations of four worksheets. These worksheets, which are also provided in the blacklines section, are used in more than one activity. They need brief preparation before use, such as titling, labeling of columns, and adding directions. When using this type of handout, the activity identifies the blackline and provides the information needed to tailor the handout for that activity.

Consider suggesting that students collect the handouts as part of a personal journal. The collection provides a good review source outside the classroom.

The choice maker as detective is a metaphor that is sparingly included throughout the book. I recommend this metaphor to your use and can say that I have found it very serviceable in teaching this material. If asked to play the role of a "choice detective," students frequently respond with enthusiasm and a freedom of expression that is not always comfortable for them as themselves. The metaphor is not applied heavily in the text, however, so that there is latitude to include personalized versions of detective activities or ignore the suggestion if desired. My use of the term "choice detective" for choice maker, the Inquiry and Investigating Procedures sections of some of the student handouts, a reflective section entitled Reflective Detective, and the dramatic activity entitled "scene investigation" are intended as light-handed suggestions for including the metaphor in your presentation of the material.

DETECTIVE METAPHOR

For each concept that uses a scene, a specific situation, setting, list of characters, and story line, some ideas for dialogue have been offered. These can be used to suit your needs. You are welcome to use them in their entirety, as a jumping off point, or not use them at all.

SCENES

Please understand that the offered lines of dialogue are provided merely to flesh out the story line. Students should not be expected to read and then memorize and deliver those lines, but rather to develop lines of their own, based on what the character might be trying to get across. It is more important for the students to understand the thoughts and feelings of the character than to reproduce a written line.

The scenes that are most beneficial to students are the scenes that most closely reflect their life experiences. You are encouraged to discard the provided scene suggestions and help your students develop scenes of their own. Or, begin with the suggested scene and follow it up with an original one. The process of creating a scene not only develops a situation that illuminates the concept being examined but also helps students thoroughly explore that concept. In addition, this builds such skills as sequencing and creative writing.

In order to develop your own scene, have students focus on the concept and determine the important aspects of that concept. Determine which event might best depict those aspects, giving preference to events that they have experienced. For example, if creating a scene that deals with anxiety, ask students: In which situations might you feel anxious? In what setting would that take place? What characters would be needed to enact that situation? What might they be thinking and doing? What would happen at the beginning, middle, and end of the scene?

The scenes are enacted simply. Use chairs and desks to represent furniture and use simple hand-held objects as necessary. Or choose to have students imagine everything. Students can move around as much or as little as is called for by the scene. When enacting the scene, it might be helpful to put the scene in the center of the room with the other students surrounding the enactment. This can foster greater group involvement.

In order to involve as many students as possible, allow several students to play the same character at different points in the scene. As students play the characters, encourage them to express the thoughts and feelings of the character through their bodies and voices. In addition to playing the characters, there are other ways students can be actively involved. For example, certain students can physically enact characters while other students voice the thoughts or feelings of those characters. Also, those not involved in the scene may be active observers, looking for nuances of body language and vocal inflection that might further illuminate the concept.

The teacher is instrumental in keeping the scene moving in its intended direction. In order to do this, either direct the scene from the outside as it evolves, or take on a main role in the scene and steer the scene through the playing of that character.

When a scene is to be enacted, the activity is shown as six steps arranged in a standard presentation format. The format is abbreviated in the activity presentation so that the suggested scene material is shown efficiently and in what is hoped is a manageable manner. I preview the format here so that I may explain and describe the steps more fully.

Step 1: Explain assumption being examined. In this step, identify for students the assumption that is being investigated. Suggested wording for the assumption is included, but please, word it to fit your class and situation.

Step 2: Develop a scene. This step includes choosing a situation, establishing setting, identifying characters, preparing roles so they reflect the assumption, and creating a story line and ideas for dialogue. Situations for studying emotional competencies abound in everyone's life; you are encouraged to solicit ideas for the scenes from students or from events that occur in their particular situation.

After deciding on the situation, choose where the situation takes place and which people are involved. For example, ask the following questions to help students develop the scene: In what kind of setting would that take place? What characters would be needed to enact the situation?

Preparing roles is the part of the activity in which students are asked to consider the effect the assumption might have on their thoughts, feelings, and actions. If they were in the situation being studied, what thoughts might go through their minds, what feelings might arise, and what behaviors might result? This part of scene development, when most successful, taps the individual student's understanding and reactions.

Creating the story line and ideas for dialogue fleshes out the scene in a prepared, although tentative, way. Ensure that the story has a beginning, middle, and end, and most important, that the end shows the results of the thoughts, feelings, and behaviors. Students come up with examples of dialogue or speech that show their own thoughts or what they think are possible thoughts, feelings, and behaviors for the situation. Stress to students that one important objective of the dialogue is for each character to voice his or her thoughts. It is very important that these ideas for dialogue serve as suggestions and as priming for students but not as lines to be memorized. What is wanted is that students understand the point the scene is trying to make and the manner in which it is being made, not that they memorize specific dialogue.

Suggestions have been provided for situation, setting, characters, role preparation, and story line with dialogue ideas. However, the scenes will apply to your students' lives more directly if you engage their personal input based on their individual experiences. Feel comfortable changing any of the scene's parameters and using suggestions in one, several, or all of the categories.

Step 3: Enact the scene. After developing a scene, students are assigned or volunteer to play specific characters, and then they act out the situation, using their own dialogue and actions. Remind them to use their bodies and voices to show what they are thinking and how they are feeling. When the thoughts are being spoken aloud, give each student an opportunity to share his or her thoughts. It is possible to increase the number of participants in a scene by having thoughts voiced aloud by one set of students while another set acts the parts. You may participate, too, if you wish.

Step 4: Reflect on the enactment. Each time a scene investigation is used to examine an assumption, a reflection on the first enactment helps students to investigate the assumption in that scene. Students do three things that help them in their scrutiny of the assumption and its results:

1. Examine assumption—examine the assumption by asking Am I crystal balling?, Am I generalizing?, and Am I awfulizing?
2. Change assumption—change the assumption into a new provable belief.
3. Act on new belief—develop and examine suggestions about how to think, feel, behave, and take action according to the new belief.

Step 5: Revise the scene. Change the scene according to the new provable belief that the students developed. Although the situation, setting, and characters remain the same as in the original scene, the thoughts, feelings, behaviors, story line, and outcomes change when the assumption changes.

Step 6: Enact the revised scene, using the new thoughts, feelings, and behaviors that the students developed. Again, remember that the ideas for dialogue serve to get the students started but are not to be a set piece for their recitation.

PART I

Choosing to
FEEL POSITIVE

CHAPTER 1

Developing Emotional Intelligence Through

SELF-AWARENESS

This chapter builds the foundation for development of emotional self-awareness. Students encounter the most important and basic concept of emotional intelligence: They choose how to think, feel, and behave.

The four lessons in this chapter introduce the basics of informed choice making. In succeeding lessons, students develop an understanding of what it means to make a choice, examine how choices may be made as a group, become aware of and investigate how emotions affect choice making, and discover how to become aware of and examine assumptions that underlie choices.

UNDERSTANDING CHOICE MAKING

Youngsters have the ability to make healthy, positive choices about how to think, feel, and behave when they are given the tools and the context to do so. Teachers have the opportunity and ability to offer both. When teachers encourage the development of their students' emotional intelligence, students will be able to apply that intelligence to the choices they make.

The development of emotional intelligence and conscious and effective choice making begins with self-awareness. Dealing with self-awareness as a global concept is a rather daunting proposition. Instead, let us start at the beginning and start small.

To make effective choices, people must first understand the definition of choice, the kinds of choices that are made, the process by which choices are made, and the ways that choices affect people. To make a *choice,* one decides what is best between two or more possibilities or alternatives. People are making choices at every moment about their every thought, feeling, and action. Often, these choices are made very quickly and below a person's level of conscious awareness. People do not know that a choice has been made or that there was the option to make other choices. Even when aware that a choice existed, a person's range of choices may be limited. Choices frequently are made by default or out of habit; are based on choices of others, such as friends, family, and the media; or are based on faulty information.

Choices lead to consequences. The accumulation of choices, whether made consciously or unconsciously, and the consequences that follow, add up to the person one is. People have the ability to design themselves as they would like to be by consciously choosing among alternatives. They can slow down their decisions and make effective, thoughtful, fact-based choices.

This lesson lays out and provides students with experience in this deliberate choice process. Students act as increasingly adept choice makers, or choice detectives, looking for facts to determine the best possible feeling, thought, and behavioral choices. Activity 1 provides a definition of choice and an opportunity for participation in the choice-making process. Activity 2 helps students understand the wide range of daily choices that they make. Activity 3 offers active analysis of the choice-making process. Activity 4 helps students gain awareness of the importance of conscious and effective choice making and elicits their commitment to becoming informed choice makers.

In addition to the actual lesson, there are many ongoing classroom opportunities for developing an awareness of and active participation in the choice-making process. Students are presented with information that each of their thoughts, feelings, and behaviors are based on a choice that they have made and for which they are responsible. Therefore, when they are demonstrating a particular thought, feeling, or behavior, students can be reminded that they are making a choice to think, feel, or act in that particular fashion. For example, if a student is feeling angry and breaking pencil points, rather than merely telling him or her to stop that behavior, remind the student that he or she is choosing to behave in that way.

Then, help the student apply the choice-making process to examine whether this was an effective choice and explore and rehearse a more effective way to deal with his or her angry feelings. In this way, the student has a structure within which to deal more appropriately with the feeling the next time it occurs (see Figure 1.1).

MAKING CHOICES

1. Look at alternatives

2. Choose an alternative

3. Act on the choice

4. Evaluate the choice

5. Keep the choice or make a new choice

Figure 1.1

This is not to say, however, that this structure will be easily applied. Choice making is based largely on habit, so youngsters need guidance at first, as well as a great deal of practice. This may seem frustrating and time-consuming at the onset of the curriculum. With practice, however, youngsters are able to make increasingly effective choices on their own, soon demanding less and less of the teacher's time. They will not need to be told to stop their ineffective behavior. Rather, they will make effective behavioral choices on their own because they know how to do so.

Students will be participating in a program that can be enjoyable and can help them to become the very best people that they can be. However, let them know that they will be experiencing new activities, some of which they may feel uncomfortable doing. If they find an activity uncomfortable, let them know that they can tell you how they feel and that they will be allowed to pass on the activity the first time it is introduced and rejoin the activity when they feel more comfortable.

Also, it may be harder for students to stay in control because of the difference between the ways in which some of these activities are structured and the regular classroom activities to which they have become accustomed. For example, they will be involved in activities in which they will be moving around as opposed to sitting in their seats. Let them know that it will be helpful if they can work hard to keep themselves in control and to ask for help when they are finding that difficult to do.

LESSON 1 Understanding Choice Making

TARGETED EMOTIONAL DOMAINS Self-Awareness

TARGETED INTELLIGENCES Verbal/Linguistic, Logical/Mathematical, Visual/Spatial, Intrapersonal, Bodily/Kinesthetic

CURRICULAR AREAS Health, Language Arts, Social Studies, Math, History

▶ Activity 1: STANDING UP FOR CHOICES

1. Explain that when making a choice, a person decides what is best out of two or more possibilities, also known as *alternatives*. Remind students that people are always making choices between alternatives. They make choices about what to believe, how to think, and how to act. Many of these choices are made without planning. It is important to plan their choices so they make the best choices possible.

2. Present two alternatives and ask students to choose one. Examples of choices to present to students:

    —Do you prefer Burger King's or McDonald's hamburgers?

    —Do you prefer sports or art?

    —In your free time, do you study or do you watch television?

    —If there was someone in class whom no one liked, would you stay away from or go up and talk to that person?

    —If you had no money and you saw some on your parent's dresser, would you take just a little bit for something you really wanted, or would you leave the money there?

    Add other choices based on your knowledge of the choices your students make. Provide a range from simple to increasingly difficult choices.

3. Students indicate their choices by standing up after their chosen alternative is read.

METACOGNITIVE DISCUSSION

Discuss with students that many choices are made without thinking. Sometimes choices are made this way because a person feels strongly about something; sometimes, because someone follows what a friend does. It is important to think before choosing so that the choice made is the best both for the chooser and other people. Informed choice makers and choice detectives make the best possible choices by slowing down and looking at available alternatives. Which choices are easy to make and which are more difficult? Who and what influences the choices that are made?

▶ Activity 2: BRAINSTORMING DAILY CHOICES

1. Explain that students are going to *brainstorm* together. Explain that brainstorming means they will search their minds for and share as many possible ideas as they can come up with about a particular topic. There are no right or wrong ideas, and they are not looking for one particular answer. Encourage them to feel free to share any idea that comes into their minds and to withhold comments about or evaluation of the ideas until a later time.

2. Students brainstorm about the daily choices that they make, those their parents make, and those their teacher makes to get an idea of the great number and variety of choices made by people every day. Examples of choices that might be identified include

   —student: what to wear, whether or not to get angry in response to a sibling's action

   —parent: what to make for dinner, whether to keep working or take a coffee break

   —teacher: whether to reprimand a student's action or let it go, how much time should be spent on a particular subject

Draw a picture of a student and discuss all the choices made during the activity, for example, choice of medium, color, whether to talk during the activity, and whether to copy someone else's idea.

METACOGNITIVE DISCUSSION

▶ Activity 3: THE CHOICE WALK

1. Ask a volunteer to walk from one side of the room to the other. Ask the rest of the class to watch very closely as the volunteer crosses the room.

2. Discuss the walk, asking what choices the person made as he or she was crossing the room. How fast did the person walk, where did the person look? Did the person think about other choices that may have been available before taking action or did the person make the choices quickly, without thinking about them? (Students will understand that the choices were made without thinking.)

3. Explain that to slow down choice making and help a person look at other possible choices, a series of choice-making steps can be used. In a way, it will be like using the pause button on the VCR before the choice is made and then making the choice in slow motion. Ask one student to walk across the room. Focus on one choice—speed when walking—to demonstrate the choice-making process:

   a. First, look at the available possibilities, that is, the alternatives. What alternatives are there in terms of speed of walking? (A person could walk slowly, at a moderate pace, quickly.)

   b. A person can then choose one of the alternatives. (Student chooses.)

   c. Explain that after a choice is made, a person can take action based on that choice. (Student walks across the room at the chosen speed.)

   d. Explain that a person can then evaluate the choice made to see whether he or she is happy with the results. (Student evaluates the choice.)

   e. If a person is not happy with the chosen alternative, a person can make a new choice and take a different action. (Student chooses whether to make a new choice.)

4. Use the list of steps for the choice-making process in Figure 1.1 to summarize for students the steps of the choice-making process.

METACOGNITIVE DISCUSSION Students analyze the process of making choices for the task of walking across the room. For example, how did the student find the alternatives? How did the student evaluate the alternatives? How did the student decide whether to change the choice?

▶ Activity 4: BECOMING INFORMED CHOICE MAKERS

1. Explain that the students may use the choice-making process, demonstrated in Activity 3 to make a simple choice of how fast to walk, to make the best choices for themselves in every area of their lives. Students can slow down their choice making and look for clues to determine the best possible choices to make.

2. Ask students to commit themselves to more deliberate choice making and the use of the choice-making process by taking a pledge. Ask each to raise his or her right hand and repeat: "I will make choices deliberately, making sure that I look for clues when choosing how I will feel, think, and act."

3. Have students design a pledge form and sign it in a collective ceremony.

Write a diary entry reflecting the daily choices made by a person in a certain period in history or the choices made by a particular historical figure or literary character being studied. — REFLECTIVE DETECTIVE

Primary Grade Modifications

STANDING UP FOR CHOICES—Modify activities to suit the interests of primary-level students. For example, go from a common and easy experience in choice making, such as deciding if one likes a food, to a common but more difficult situation, such as when one wants a toy that a friend is using or when one is angry with and hits a sibling.

BRAINSTORMING DAILY CHOICES—Take a more active role in the activities, demonstrating the concepts as students follow. For example, focus only on the choices made by the students and give examples first, such as wearing a dress or pants, eating toast or cereal, smiling or frowning, yelling or talking in quiet voices, listening or not paying attention, raising hands or talking out loud.

Middle and High School Modifications

STANDING UP FOR CHOICES—Add examples, such as, "If someone offered you a drink at a party, would you take it?" "If you had not studied for a test and could see someone's paper out of the corner of your eye, would you look?" "If you were pressured to do something you were uncomfortable doing or if you did not, you would lose a friend, would you do it?"

BRAINSTORMING DAILY CHOICES—Focus on the choices students were able to make in the past, the choices they can make now, and the choices they will be able to make in the future. Give examples of past choices—what to eat, what to wear; of present choices—what activities to do, what to do on a date, where to apply to college; of future choices—who to marry, where to live, where to work. Students might write and deliver a speech entitled "The Effects of Geographic Location and Economic Status on the Range of Choices Available to Us."

DEVELOPING GROUP CHOICE MAKING

Lesson 1 provided students with a basic awareness of the choice-making process and how it affects them. Lesson 2 helps students generalize that awareness to how their choices affect others and how group choices occur. Students begin developing an understanding of and experience in cooperation and develop a set of rules to govern their behavior.

Examining and experiencing the process by which collective choices are made lays the foundation for the development of several emotional domains. Students expand their knowledge of the choice-making process and begin to practice self-control and management of their emotions. Understanding the importance of and joy in the search for ways to make choices that benefit the greatest number of people develops the foundation for empathy and for handling relationships.

Exploring group choice making in a school context necessitates that one acknowledge the inherent hierarchical setup of a classroom. A class is not a democracy by nature. The teacher is responsible for a relatively large group of youngsters in a setting that demands certain kinds of behaviors but rejects others. It is a setting that requires that the teacher transmit a great deal of information in a few short hours. Therefore, the teacher makes choices for the group, setting schedule and rules so teaching may be effective. Students are expected to adhere to the rules and cooperate with the teacher and each other. They receive a strong message that they are expected to obey authority.

Although this is an important message, it is not necessarily the only one that it is desirable to teach students. Nor is it necessarily the best message with which to encourage cooperation and positive behavior. Teaching the meaning and benefits of cooperation and eliciting participation in the development of classroom rules sends the message that students know what is necessary for a smooth-running classroom and are capable of doing it. The act of developing those rules is an opportunity to explore necessary behaviors as well as actively experience group choice making.

There are several ways in which the group choice-making process can occur (see Figure 1.2).

HOW GROUP CHOICES ARE MADE	
Authority	One person in charge makes choices for the whole group.
Consensus	Each person in the group agrees on the choice.
Majority	More than one-half of the people in the group agree on the choice.

Figure 1.2

SkyLight Training and Publishing Inc.

A choice can be made for a group through the use of *authority.* In this situation, one person in charge chooses and imposes the choice on the group. There may be several rules in your classroom that are nonnegotiable and that would be decided in this way. It would be helpful to explain to your students why this is so and the reasons behind the rules, such as safety, state laws, and so forth.

A choice can be reached by group *consensus.* This means that every person in the group agrees on the choice before it is acted on. An example of a group choice made in this way would be one made by a jury in which all jurors had to agree on a verdict.

Also, a choice can be reached by a *majority* of the group members agreeing on it. An example of this would be an election for class officers. There may be several rules that can be decided upon by students by majority or consensus, offering active participation in the group choice-making process.

It will be helpful for students to understand that working together well, or *cooperating,* can make a group more enjoyable and each person in it happier. However, to cooperate is a choice that each individual group member must make. It is not always easy to cooperate because it sometimes means that one has to wait one's turn, share something that one is enjoying, or agree to something to which one would rather not agree. However, the benefits of cooperation are that each person is guaranteed a turn at some point, all group members are expected to share, and there are many times when one's idea would be the group's choice. When members exercise some self-control and tolerate some frustration, the group works well, accomplishes great things, and is an enjoyable experience for each of its members.

The activities in Lesson 2 explore these areas of cooperation and group choice making. Activity 1 offers an experience in and an understanding of the benefits of cooperation. Activity 2 elicits participation in the development of group rules. Activity 3 presents an opportunity to make a group decision about the rules that will govern classroom behavior as well as how they are implemented.

In addition to the actual lesson, other opportunities can be found for encouraging cooperation, reinforcing skills, and helping to improve the classroom atmosphere. The entire class can encourage responsibility by classmates for effective choice making. Students can be taught to help each other use the choice-making process to examine choices and to offer alternatives, and they can support each other for positive choices made.

LESSON 2

Developing Group Choice Making

TARGETED EMOTIONAL DOMAINS Self-Awareness, Self-Control, Empathy, Handling Relationships

TARGETED INTELLIGENCES Verbal/Linguistic, Logical/Mathematical, Visual/Spatial, Bodily/Kinesthetic, Musical/Rhythmic, Intrapersonal, Interpersonal

CURRICULAR AREAS Health, Language Arts, Social Studies, Math, Music

▶ Activity 1: ALPHABET

1. Before starting, create a space in which the students can move about freely.

2. Explain that you will call out a letter and that every one in the class will join to make a physical picture of the letter. To do this, students stand up and move together to form the letter as quickly as possible. However, tell students that they may not speak while forming the letter! They are to form the letters as a group, in silence.

3. Begin with simply shaped letters such as T and O and gradually move on to more complex shapes such as N and R.

METACOGNITIVE DISCUSSION

Discuss with students how the letters were formed. What did they have to do in order to make it work? What would have made it more difficult? Students may use the word *cooperation*. Encourage them to be specific in terms of the ways in which they cooperated. For example, perhaps a student looked for a part of a letter not yet formed and went to that place or one student took another student and placed him or her in an available spot. If students fought for the same spot, it would have made the activity more difficult to accomplish.

▶ Activity 2: BRAINSTORMING GROUP RULES

1. Students are going to make a group choice about the kinds of rules they think are needed in order to work together smoothly as a group. Tell them that their choices affect other people. It is important to make choices that have the best effect on the most people.

2. Ask students to brainstorm as many rules as they think they will need. You may give general areas in which rules may be needed, such as disruptive

behaviors, noise level, or ways to participate. Ask for a student volunteer to record the rules that are suggested. An example of some rules that might be suggested:

—No one may put down anyone in the class.

—Everyone will listen to instructions.

—No one will speak when another person is speaking.

—If the noise level becomes too high, a signal will be given and will be followed by silence.

—Everyone will be in charge of keeping themselves in control.

Ask students to turn the brainstorm list into a song by coming up with a melody of their own or by putting the words to a song that they already know.

METACOGNITIVE DISCUSSION

▶ Activity 3: RULES VOTE

1. Explain that although rules may often be decided by someone in authority, in order to make their group choice about the kinds of rules they want, the students will vote, inviting everyone to participate in the choice-making process and allowing the majority to make the final choice.

2. Explain that you will read their list of rules, and they are to raise their hand to vote to include that rule. They may vote for as many rules as they think they need. As the rules are voted upon, ask the recorder to list the accepted rules so that the list may be posted as a reminder. Give a copy of The Cooperation Rules We Choose by Majority (see Blacklines) to students and suggest they record the rules for their own journals.

3. Explain that the students have just participated in the choice-making process. They looked at the alternatives available and chose the alternatives they wanted. However, the process is not yet complete. The next step is acting on the choices they made. They are in charge of acting according to the rules they chose. This may mean that they will need to remind themselves and their classmates of the rules that were chosen, when they have forgotten to follow them for the moment. Also, after acting according to the rules for a period of time, they may want to evaluate the rules they chose and change them if they think changes are necessary.

Ask students to write and deliver a speech as an expert about one of the group choice-making methods. For example, they might consider the way a jury reaches

REFLECTIVE DETECTIVE

a verdict (consensus), the way in which a president is voted into office (majority), or the way in which the constitution was developed (majority).

Primary Grade Modifications

Explain that cooperation means working well together. Eliminate examples of choices made by authority, consensus, and majority if they are beyond the comprehension level of the students.

ALPHABET—Use shapes instead of letters if students are not yet reading. For example, have them create a square, triangle, or flower.

BRAINSTORMING GROUP RULES—Have students first share the classroom rules already in place and discuss who made those rules and who follows them. Then, giving examples first, ask students to come up with additional rules they think might be needed. The song may be eliminated, or help your students put the rules to a well-known tune such as "Old MacDonald." You might demonstrate role-playing by acting out one of the chosen rules so they can see what the rule looks like in action.

Middle and High School Modifications

Ask students to give examples of choices made by consensus, authority, and majority and discuss the benefits and problems with each method.

ALPHABET—If students catch on quickly, have them make letters within a certain time limit or create words and sentences.

BRAINSTORMING GROUP RULES—Ask students to brainstorm implicit rules, such as social rules between peers, as well as rules that are currently in place that they believe should be modified or eliminated. Students might then work in small groups to develop songs, jingles, or raps. A good follow-up for this activity is to ask students to create a time line, detailing the rules one has to follow as a child, a teenager, and then as an adult.

IDENTIFYING FEELINGS

In order to be able to manage emotions, which leads to greater emotional intelligence and more effective choice making, a person must first be aware that emotions exist. At every moment, one is experiencing a particular feeling or combination of feelings. Often, these feelings inhabit a person's being with little awareness or conscious choice by the person. They affect people in many ways, including their physiology, movement, and speech. The ways people are affected by their feelings and how those feelings are expressed vary widely from person to person.

Without realizing it, feelings propel people to act to change them, remove them, or keep them. This can lead to choices that bring no result, the opposite result, or results not in a person's best interests. With increased awareness of feelings and how to respond to them, a person begins to move toward conscious and effective choice. People can work toward choosing and rehearsing how they would like to feel and how to express their feelings.

First, however, a person needs to become aware that he or she is experiencing an emotion and to look to his or her body for clues as to the nature of that emotion. Bodies and voices provide those clues (see Figure 1.3).

HOW TO KNOW WHAT ONE IS FEELING

How parts of the body are held

Posture

Tension

Gestures

Facial expressions

Eye contact

Voice rate

Voice pitch

Voice volume

Figure 1.3

Lesson 3 focuses on identifying feelings. Its activities help students to identify emotions they are experiencing. Activity 1 reinforces cooperation. Activity 2 presents an opportunity for students to connect an imagined situation to its corresponding feeling. Activity 3 gives students a chance to experience and identify a variety of feelings in their bodies. In Activity 4, students communicate a variety of emotional messages with their bodies alone.

SkyLight Training and Publishing Inc.

In addition to the lesson, there are other opportunities for identifying feelings in the classroom. You may act as a model for your students, sharing your feelings in whatever way you are comfortable. Also, identify body language that is observed in students, offering them the opportunity to discuss their feelings should they choose to do so.

LESSON 3

Identifying Feelings

TARGETED EMOTIONAL DOMAINS   Self-Awareness, Managing Emotions

TARGETED INTELLIGENCES   Verbal /Linguistic, Visual/Spatial, Bodily/Kinesthetic, Intrapersonal, Naturalist

CURRICULAR AREAS   Health, Social Studies, Language Arts, Science

▶ Activity 1: ALPHABET

Do the same activity as in Lesson 2, Activity 1. For metacognitive discussion, ask students what specific things they did or did not do in order to form the letters. Was it different than the first time they did this? How?

▶ Activity 2: "HOW WOULD YOU FEEL IF . . ."

1. Explain that people are always feeling a certain way, such as happy, sad, or angry. Sometimes, people know what they are feeling and why, and sometimes they do not. It is important for them to be aware of how they feel so they can choose how they want to feel and how best to deal with those feelings. People show their feelings in different ways, for example, by the looks on their faces, how they speak, and how they act. They can choose how they would like to feel and how they show their feelings. The first step is paying attention to how they are feeling right now. They can do this by looking at their bodies and listening to their voices.

2. Explain that you are going to make a number of different statements. Ask students to listen to the statement and imagine how they would feel if the statement was meant for them, personally. Examples of statements that might be used

   —I am so proud of you.

   —Your work is improving nicely.

—You have five more minutes to complete the test.

—The doctor will see you now.

—I'll be your best friend if you give me some of your candy.

—I don't think I'll ever be able to trust you again.

—Nobody likes you.

—You can never do anything right.

—I've got your book bag and I'm not going to give it back.

3. Ask students to share some of the feelings they experienced as they listened to the statements. How did they know they were experiencing those feelings?

▶ Activity 3: FEELINGS GAUGE

1. Ask students to stand up and allow for a little elbow room between themselves.

2. Explain that you will call out a series of different feelings. After you call out a feeling, the students are going to imagine what their bodies might be going through if they were experiencing that feeling. Then, starting at the top of their heads and moving down to their toes, they are to act out that feeling with each part of their bodies. Examples of feelings that you might use are sadness, joy, anger, surprise, or fear.

Ask students to focus on the way in which parts of the body are held, tension, facial expressions, eye contact, gestures, and posture.

METACOGNITIVE DISCUSSION

▶ Activity 4: MESSAGES

1. Explain that people can tell a great deal about how they and others are feeling by paying attention to their bodies. Often, they give messages to each other using only their bodies.

2. Tell students that you will be call out a series of messages. After you call out a message, the students will "say" that message using only their bodies. (Have one-half the class stand and one-half sit so that students see that body language exists regardless of position.) They can use the way in which they hold different parts of their bodies, tension, facial expressions, eye contact, gestures, and posture, but they may not speak. Examples of messages that might be used include

—I'm so tired.

—I'm bored.

—I didn't do anything wrong!

—Please let me answer the question.

—I'm very proud of you.

—I can't believe you just said that!

—One more word out of you and you've had it!

—I'm so nervous.

—Please don't look at me.

—See how wonderful I look.

3. Ask students what other messages they give and receive. Did everyone give the same message in the same way? What were some of the similarities and differences between the ways in which the messages were given?

REFLECTIVE
DETECTIVE

A good follow-up activity for this lesson is to have students help each other outline their bodies on a large piece of paper. Then, each student chooses a feeling and colors the parts of their body outline that are affected by that feeling. Remind them to include facial expressions, muscles, heart rate, pulse, and so forth.

Primary Grade Modifications

HOW WOULD YOU FEEL IF . . . ?—Use examples, such as "I like you," "It's not your turn," "You're mean," and "There is nothing under your bed."

FEELINGS GAUGE—Demonstrate first. Ask students to make a feelings collage out of pictures cut from magazines and their own drawings.

MESSAGES—Demonstrate first.

Middle and High School Modifications

Ask students for specific examples of the ways in which their feelings are expressed in their bodies, voices, and actions.

HOW WOULD YOU FEEL IF . . . ?—Add examples such as "He thinks you're cute," "I'm ashamed to call you my son," "I don't care what your curfew is, I want you home by 11:00!"

FEELINGS GAUGE—As a feeling is expressed, have students freeze, look around, and describe the specific similarities and differences in the way the feelings are expressed.

MESSAGES—Have students add their own examples of messages they give each other and those that are given to them.

In order to truly make and execute effective choices, it is not enough to simply understand the definition of choice making. One must understand the basis for one's choices. Lesson 4 illuminates choice making at that fundamental level at which choices are truly made—one's underlying beliefs.

UNDERSTANDING ASSUMPTIONS

The choices made in one's life are based on unquestioned assumptions. These assumptions are beliefs, but not provable facts. These assumptions inform thoughts, lead to feelings, and motivate actions. However, the assumption-thought-feeling chain happens so quickly that a person is rarely aware that it occurs. Because it is beneath conscious awareness, it becomes difficult or almost impossible to influence any part of the chain to make a different choice.

In order to make more effective choices, it is necessary to become aware of the assumptions, evaluating them for exaggerations and other errors in logic. Then, a person can change the assumptions to provable beliefs, alter the corresponding thoughts and feelings, and explore and rehearse new choices based on them. The first step in this process is understanding the basic nature of assumptions, which Lesson 4 clarifies. Ellis (1990) identified three concerns when examining assumptions (see Figure 1.4). These concerns, couched as three questions for student deliberation, open a previously closed assumption to fresh consideration.

There are three basic errors in logic that lead to assumptions. One error in logic is *crystal balling*. This is when someone wrongly claims to know what will

---

CONCERNS FOR EXAMINING ASSUMPTIONS

Am I crystal balling?—When one claims to know what will happen in the future.

Am I generalizing?—When one exaggerates and stretches the truth.

Am I awfulizing?—When one claims that something is awful, terrible, or horrible.

Based on A. Ellis, *How to Stubbornly Refuse to Make Yourself Miserable About Anything, Yes, Anything*, 1990, (New York: First Carol).

Figure 1.4

---

happen in the future. Clearly, it is stretching the truth to believe that one can predict the future exactly. However, someone might steer clear of new activities because he or she is sure he or she would do badly. If this assumption is rewritten to a provable belief, a person could then see a realm of future possibilities. The person might do badly, but there is also the possibility that he or she would be average or even good at the new activity.

Another error is *generalizing,* or exaggerating the truth. An example of this would be people believing that everybody has to like them. It is stretching the realm of possibility to believe that every single person in the world has to like them. This may seem logical and obvious on paper. However, many assumptions and choices are based on hanging on to this kind of thinking, despite its inherent lack of logic.

For example, a belief in the assumption that everybody must like you might lead to constantly agreeing to do things for other people despite personal situations, such as lack of time. If you were to say no, someone might not like you and you would feel that that would be intolerable. Or would it? Look at the facts and not the beliefs, and rewrite the assumption to make more sense. You might prefer that most people like you, but it is stretching the truth to believe that everybody must. The worst thing that might happen is some people might not like you. You might not be thrilled about that but you could tolerate it.

The third basic error in logic is *awfulizing,* or claiming that something is awful, horrible, or terrible. If one looks at outcomes on an awfulness scale, it is logical that more negative weight might be put on situations dealing with factually bad circumstances, such as bad health or death. However, sometimes, something is labeled as awful when the situation is less than awful. It is really just a situation that is not liked. This may lead to a variety of negative feelings, clearly out of proportion to the situation. How many of us have hyperventilated and wasted valuable down time while stuck in traffic?

Activities in Lesson 4 provide students with the opportunity to become acquainted with these errors in logic. Activity 1 provides additional opportunity for experiencing and examining cooperation. Activity 2 further builds awareness of the effects of emotions in one's body, and Activity 3 develops an awareness of the effects of emotions on one's voice. Activity 4 highlights the difference between facts and beliefs. Activity 5 offers experiential opportunity to explore assumptions and their effects on bodies, voices, and choices. Activity 6 provides information about the basic errors in logic and provable beliefs, and Activity 7 provides an experiential opportunity to apply that information.

In addition to the lesson, it would be helpful to explore assumptions behind students' actions when an occasion arises in class. Rather than merely correcting a behavior, explore the assumption that led to that behavior. For example, if a student were throwing homework away before it was completed, explore the possibility that the student was awfulizing and held the assumption that the homework had to be perfect. Work toward an understanding that imperfection is not awful and that attempts, even failed attempts, are worthwhile and important steps in learning.

Understanding Assumptions

LESSON

4

TARGETED EMOTIONAL DOMAINS Self-Awareness, Managing Emotions

TARGETED INTELLIGENCES Verbal/Linguistic, Visual/Spatial, Logical/Mathematical, Bodily/Kinesthetic, Intrapersonal, Interpersonal, Naturalist

CURRICULAR AREAS Health, Social Studies, Language Arts, Math, Science

▶ Activity 1: ALPHABET

Do the same activity as in Lesson 2, Activity 1. Try a few letters, with the students acting as if they are experiencing a number of different emotions. For meta-cognitive discussion, ask students how they feel when they are cooperating. How do they feel when they are not cooperating? How might this activity be affected if they were feeling angry? How might this activity be affected if they were feeling shy?

▶ Activity 2: SIT/STAND

1. Explain that, as learned in the previous lesson, the way a person feels affects his or her body. People even express how they feel by the way they stand up and sit down.

2. Tell students that you are going to ask them to stand and sit as if they are thinking a number of different thoughts and feeling a number of different feelings. They are to stand and sit, showing what they are thinking and feeling using only their bodies. Examples that might be used include

   —Sit as if you really wanted to be out of your seat and running around.

   —Sit as if you were on a throne.

   —Sit as if you did not want anyone to see you.

   —Stand as if your name was just called in class and you did not know the answer.

   —Stand as if you were a finalist in a pageant, and the winner's name was about to be called.

   —Stand as if you were threatening someone.

3. Have the students focus on the way the body is held, tension, energy, and so forth.

► Activity 3: SUBTEXT

1. Explain to students that feelings not only affect a person's body, but they affect one's voice as well. People use their voices in different ways to deliver different meanings.

2. Tell students that you are going to call out several phrases and several meanings for those phrases. After you count to three, they are to say the phrase together, using their voices to get across the different meanings. Have the students focus on rate of speech, pitch, and volume. Examples of things to say:

   —Say "I'm sorry" as if you are being coerced to say it by a parent.

   —Say "I'm sorry" as if you have just stepped on your best friend's foot.

   —Say "Who, me?" as if you've just won a million dollars in the lottery.

   —Say "Who, me?" as if you've been asked to answer a question on an oral exam for which you have not studied.

3. Ask students how the rate of speech, pitch, and volume changed meanings. What sentences could they add to the phrases that would tell what else they are saying in addition to the phrase itself? For example, in the first meaning of "I'm sorry," you might be saying, "I'm not really sorry. I'm being made to say this to you."

► Activity 4: BELIEF VOTE

1. Explain to students that choices made about feelings, thoughts, and actions are based on beliefs. *Beliefs* are things that a person thinks are true but which may or may not be true in fact. Things that may not be true are also called *assumptions*. It is important to know that one's beliefs are true and are based on fact so one can make the best possible choices. People search for facts to do this.

2. Tell students that you will first tell them two possible beliefs and then call out the beliefs one at a time. They are to choose one belief, making their choice by standing up after you call out the one they choose. Examples of choices might be

   —McDonald's hamburgers are the best or Burger King's hamburgers are the best.

   —The moon is made of green cheese or the moon is not made of green cheese.

   —The earth is flat or the earth is round.

   —The United States is the best place to live or Canada is the best place to live.

3. Ask students how they chose which hamburger was better. Are our choices influenced by anyone other than ourselves? Who and what might influence our choices? How do we know the makeup of the moon? Did people always know that? How do we know the shape of the earth? What choice might have been made several centuries ago? What influence do available facts have on choices made? Which choice do they think that someone living in Toronto, Canada, might have made about the best place to live? What influence does personal experience have on choices made?

▶ Activity 5: ASSUMPTION WALK

1. Divide the class into two groups and have the groups stand on opposite sides of the room. Clear a path so that students can cross from one side of the room to the other. (Have only one group walk for this activity and use the second group for Activity 7.)

2. Explain that you are going to tell one group an assumption that will be a secret from the other group. Use the assumption "When I cross the room, everyone will look at me and think I look stupid, and that will be awful." After the group hears the assumption, they walk halfway across the room, expressing that assumption with their faces and bodies as they walk.

3. They stop in the center of the room and say "hello" in a way that expresses that assumption through their voices. They then cross the rest of the way, still expressing that assumption through their bodies.

4. As the group crosses, the other group tries to determine what the assumption is, looking for the specific ways in which that assumption is expressed through body and voice.

▶ Activity 6: EXAMINING ASSUMPTIONS

1. Help students think about the *crystal ball* assumption by asking "Am I crystal balling?" Explain that crystal balling is when a person claims to know exactly what will happen in the future. An example of this was the first group's assumption in which group members claimed to know that others would think that they were stupid. Explain that it is impossible to predict exactly what will happen in the future and that doing this is not based on facts. There is a possibility that others might think that a person is stupid, but beliefs are based on proof, not possibilities. There are many other possibilities as well. Others might not think anything at all about the person as a result of his or her walk, or they may think that he or she looked great. One cannot predict what may happen in the future.

2. Help students examine the *generalizing* assumption by asking "Am I generalizing?" Explain that generalizing is to exaggerate or stretch the truth. An example of this was the first group's assumption that everyone would think that they were stupid. Explain that it is stretching the truth to believe that every single person in the class is thinking the same thing and that it is not based on facts to think that everyone is thinking the same thing. There is a possibility that some might think that they were stupid, but they are to remember that provable beliefs are based on proof and not possibilities.

3. Help students examine the *awfulizing* assumption by asking "Am I awfulizing?" Explain that awfulizing is stretching the truth by claiming that something is awful, terrible, or horrible. An example of this was the first group's assumption that being thought of as stupid by others would be awful.

   Explain that it is usually exaggerating to believe that something is awful, terrible, or horrible and that the belief is not based on facts. A person might prefer not being called stupid, but beliefs are based on facts, not exaggerations. The worst thing that may happen if someone is called stupid is that the person may not like it. However, no one can prove that this would be awful.

▶ Activity 7: PROVABLE BELIEF WALK

1. Remind students that the first group's assumption was unprovable.

2. Do Activity 5 again, using the second group for the walk. Give them a provable belief that is not based on crystal balling, generalizing, or awfulizing (use "When I cross the room, some people might look at me.").

3. Ask students to reflect on the differences they saw in the two groups' behaviors during their walks. Ask them if they think making an assumption affects their behavior.

REFLECTIVE DETECTIVE
A good follow-up activity is to suggest that the students write about scientific assumptions that, based on new evidence, have changed over time.

Primary Grade Modifications

SIT/STAND—Demonstrate activity first.

SUBTEXT—Demonstrate first and take a more active role in the follow-up discussion.

BELIEF VOTE—Take a more active role in the follow-up discussion.

ASSUMPTION WALK—Give the assumption aloud and have the rest of the class choose how the group should walk and talk based on options you provide. For example, how do they think they should stand, straight or bent? Where do they think their eyes would be looking, down or straight ahead? Do they think they would walk quickly or slowly? Would they say hello softly or loudly?

EXAMINING ASSUMPTIONS—Elaborate if necessary and have students repeat definitions of crystal balling, generalizing, and awfulizing aloud.

PROVABLE BELIEF WALK—Modify as for Assumption Walk.

REFLECTIVE DETECTIVE—An excellent follow-up activity might be to have students dance a variety of feelings.

Middle and High School Modifications

ALPHABET—Have students discuss the specific ways the activity changed as the emotions changed. Discuss the ways in which other kinds of activities might be similarly affected.

SIT/STAND—Have students discuss the specific ways the movements were affected by the circumstances.

SUBTEXT—Have students provide specific examples of the effect of subtext in their daily lives.

ASSUMPTION WALK—Have students discuss other assumptions that affect the way we enter a room and carry ourselves.

EXAMINING ASSUMPTIONS—Have students offer personal examples of crystal balling, generalizing, and awfulizing.

PROVABLE BELIEF WALK—Have students discuss the contexts in which changing assumptions and the ways in which we carry ourselves would be beneficial.

CHAPTER 2

Developing Emotional Intelligence Through

MANAGING EMOTIONS

This chapter offers opportunities for students to apply their understanding of the choice-making process. Using their knowledge of the assumption-thought-feeling-action chain, students examine effective choices across a wide range of situations.

The five lessons in this chapter explore assumptions believed and choices made regarding three emotions (anxiety, anger, and happiness) and two issues influencing emotions (hiding feelings and responsibility). They offer opportunities for building emotional intelligence in the areas of self-awareness, managing emotions, and self-control. Awareness of how one is feeling can lead to a choice about when, how, and how intensely one would like to experience that emotion and how one would like to deal with it.

EXAMINING AND LOWERING ANXIETY

Anxiety is an emotion based partly on the assumption "If something seems fearsome, I must get terribly upset." When a person believes this particular assumption and applies it across a wide range of situations, that person can spend quite a bit of time feeling anxious.

It can be helpful to look at the physiological origins of anxiety. Human beings and other animals are given the ability to find a great amount of energy and strength with which to run away from or fight a perceived danger. People experience this energy in the form of adrenaline; their hearts go faster and they perspire. In prehistoric times, this energy gave the cave dwellers a chance to survive by fighting off or escaping from such dangers as saber-toothed tigers.

Often, however, people respond to fairly safe situations as if the situation were as dangerous as an attack by saber-toothed tigers and fill their bodies with the kind of energy it would take to fight off that kind of danger. Not all situations are that dangerous nor do they all call for that amount of energy. By examining the assumption and thoughts related to anxiety, people teach themselves not to respond automatically. Students begin to understand that they have the choice to feel many ways about situations, not just terribly upset, and that not all situations are awful or horrible. They can determine the level of danger and find the right amount of energy with which to respond.

The activities in Lesson 5 examine assumptions believed and choices made with regard to anxiety. Activity 1 helps students examine the physiological responses to anxiety, building their awareness of when they are feeling this emotion. Activity 2 increases awareness of situations that trigger anxiety. Activity 3 provides experience in examining one's thoughts. Activity 4 teaches students a useful relaxation technique. Activity 5 provides an opportunity to explore the assumption that leads to anxiety by developing and enacting a dramatic scene based on the assumption.

In addition to these activities, there are other ways of becoming aware of and lowering anxiety. Students can be encouraged to explore their feelings at stressful times such as exams. Also, by offering them opportunities to practice in class you can encourage them to use relaxation techniques on a regular basis.

Examining and Lowering Anxiety

LESSON 5

TARGETED EMOTIONAL DOMAINS Self-Awareness, Managing Emotions

TARGETED INTELLIGENCES Verbal/Linguistic, Visual/Spatial, Logical/Mathematical, Bodily/Kinesthetic, Musical/Rhythmic, Intrapersonal

CURRICULAR AREAS Health, Social Studies, Language Arts, Math

▶ Activity 1: BRAINSTORMING STRESS INDICATORS

1. Explain that there are times when people may feel nervous or anxious, such as when they have a big test coming up or when they have to get a shot at the doctor's. It is important for them to look at their bodies and listen to their voices in order to identify that they are feeling anxious.

2. Ask students to brainstorm the physical things that their bodies and their voices do when they are anxious and express those things through movement. Examples of things that they might suggest include stuttering, shaky voice, shaking body, sweating, stomachache, headache, or forgetting.

▶ Activity 2: INQUIRY

1. Prepare the Anxiety Check form by using the two column with scale format (see Blacklines). Write the title at the top of the page. Label the columns *Day* and *Amount of Anxiety*. Add the directions: "Fill in the day and show the amount of anxiety you feel on the scale." Add the word *Anxiety* to each scale value.

2. Ask students to complete the inquiry sentence—"I am anxious when . . . ." on the Anxiety handout (see Blacklines).

3. Introduce the Anxiety Check form at the end of the lesson and ask students to fill it out during the week.

▶ Activity 3: SELF-TALK

1. Explain that people are always thinking about something, even when they are not aware of it.

2. Ask students to sit silently and close their eyes for one minute. During that time, ask them to pay close attention to all the thoughts going through their minds.

3. After a minute, ask who would like to share one of the thoughts they were able to catch. (Have the students share several examples.)

4. Explain to students that the thoughts they think lead to the feelings they feel. For example, certain thoughts can lead to feelings of anxiety. Ask students to imagine that a very important test is about to be given and that they do not feel prepared. Have students sit silently and close their eyes for a minute. During that time, they are to pay close attention to all the thoughts that might be going through their minds, knowing that an important test is about to begin.

5. Ask who would like to share one of the thoughts they were able to catch. (Have the students share several examples.) Examples they might share include

   —I'm going to flunk this one.

   —I wish I could get out of here.

   —I knew I should have studied.

   —I had better hide my report card when it comes out.

▶ Activity 4: RAGS

Note: This activity is an excellent relaxer. Use it when students need to loosen up and unwind.

1. Have the students stand with enough room in front of them to bend over. Explain that this exercise helps them relax their bodies.

2. Ask them to imagine that the muscles in their bodies are slowly changing to rags. Beginning with the top of their heads and slowly moving down their backs, they are to imagine that one muscle group at a time is going to disappear and be replaced with a collection of limp rags.

3. Because rags cannot hold up any part of a body, when that body part has changed to rags, allow it to hang loosely. When their bodies through their backs are made entirely of rags, ask them to hang limply for a few seconds, paying close attention to the sensation of being made of rags rather than muscles.

4. After hanging, ask them to return to standing, very slowly, by adding just enough muscle to the rags in order to get themselves to stand, but no more than is absolutely needed. Have them try to fill their body with a mixture of rags and muscles.

5. Ask students what it felt like to be made of rags. Was it more difficult for a certain part of their bodies to turn into rags? When do they think they might be able to use this exercise?

6. Tell students that the rags exercise also can be done sitting in a chair and that there is no need to hang all the way over to feel the sensation of rags. The exercise also can be used to focus on a particularly tense part of the body, such as a hand that is holding a pencil too tightly.

▶ Activity 5: SCENE INVESTIGATION: STRESSING OUT

1. Explain to students that they are to develop and act a scene to examine the assumption

THE ASSUMPTION

> "If something seems fearsome, I must
> get terribly upset."

Create a suitable scene, using the lesson scene as an example.

2. Develop a scene:

CHOOSE A SITUATION taking a test

ESTABLISH SETTING a classroom

IDENTIFY CHARACTERS students and a teacher

PREPARE ROLES TO REFLECT ASSUMPTION

Thoughts

—I'll never do well.

—I'm going to fail.

—I won't remember anything.

—I'm going to be killed if I don't do well.

—My life will be over.

Feelings

—nervous, stressed, hopeless, or sad

Behaviors

—asking to leave the class to go to the washroom

—acting up by throwing an eraser

—looking at someone else's paper

—fidgeting with the pencil

CREATE A STORY LINE AND IDEAS FOR DIALOGUE

EXAMPLE STORY LINE
"STRESSING OUT"

> The teacher announces that an important test is about to begin. The teacher says, "Class, please put your books in your desks and take out a pencil. You are about to take a very important math test."
>
> Students speak their thoughts aloud. "I'm going to fail. I'm going to get into trouble." One student asks to leave the room, another throws an eraser while another fidgets with a pencil. "May I please be excused?"
>
> The test is given out. Students attempt to fill in the answers, with very little to no success.
>
> The teacher briefly looks over the tests and tells the class that she is very disappointed with the results. "I looked over the results and I'm afraid that no one did well. I'm very disappointed because I know you could have done better."

3. Enact the scene: Students choose parts and act out the scene, using their own thoughts, dialogue, and behaviors.

4. Reflect on the enactment:

THE ASSUMPTION
EXAMINED

EXAMINE ASSUMPTION Remind students that the assumption was "If something seems fearsome, I must get terribly upset." Students ask three questions:

Am I crystal balling?

The assumption says that a person knows with certainty that something will happen in the future that is to be feared. Informed choice makers know that it is impossible to predict that something that seems fearsome is truly something to fear. Something that seems fearsome may or may not be something to fear.

Am I generalizing?

The assumption says that there is no other possible choice but to get terribly upset. Informed choice makers know that using the word *must* is an example of exaggerating. *Must* means that there is no choice, that a person could not live without getting terribly upset. But the fact is that the only things one must have to live are things related to physical safety, such as air, water, and food. A person may feel, at the moment, that he or she has no other choice and must become terribly upset, and then the person allows him- or herself to feel this way. However, after examining the assumption, the person realizes that he or she does not have to feel terribly upset, that he or she has the choice to feel many other ways.

Am I awfulizing?

The assumption says that something that seems fearful is awful and horrible and cause for becoming terribly upset. An informed choice maker knows that it is stretching the truth to believe that everything that seems fearsome is reason for being terribly upset. In certain situations, there may be some reason for concern that could lead a person to take action with regard to what seems fearsome. However, all situations do not demand that one become terribly upset.

CHANGE ASSUMPTION The new belief is

THE PROVABLE
BELIEF

> "If something seems fearsome, I do not have
> to get terribly upset."

ACT ON NEW BELIEF To adjust to the new provable belief, students consider the following:

Feeling

—Observe their bodies and ask themselves what they are feeling, for example, anxiety.

Thinking

—Observe their thoughts and ask themselves to identify their self-talk. For example, "There is something to fear and I am terribly upset. I have no choice to feel any other way."

Behaving

—Change their self-talk to go along with the revised belief. "Something seems fearsome, but I do not have to get terribly upset. The worst thing that could happen would be that I would have to take the test over again, and that wouldn't be so bad."

Take Action

—If something is truly dangerous, they can leave the situation or get help. If it is not, they can change their belief and their self-talk, and they can do something to help their body relax.

5. Revise the scene:

PREPARE ROLES TO REFLECT NEW BELIEF

Thoughts

—I might do well on this test. If I don't do well, the worst that could happen is that I'd have to take it again. I'll try to remember what I was taught.

Feelings

—hope, anticipation

Behaviors

—One student does the rags exercise, others quietly think through the subject matter, while others think through their positive self-talk.

CREATE A STORY LINE AND IDEAS FOR DIALOGUE

EXAMPLE STORY LINE
"STRESSING OUT"
REVISED SCENE

> The teacher announces that an important test is about to begin. "Class, please put your books in your desks and take out a pencil. You are about to take a very important math test."
>
> Students speak their thoughts out loud. "I might do well on this test. I'll try to remember what I was taught." One student does the rags exercise, others quietly think through the subject matter while others think through their positive self-talk.
>
> The test is given out, and students fill out most of the answers.
>
> The teacher briefly looks over the test and tells the class how proud she is. "I looked over the results, and I see that most of you have done well. I watched you while you were taking the test, and I am most proud of the fact that every one of you used your choice detective skills and tried your very best."

6. Students act out the revised scene, using their bodies and voices to show what they are thinking and how they are feeling.

REFLECTIVE
DETECTIVE

Create and perform two brief songs with movement—one on anxiety and one on keeping calm. Use material from this lesson for movement and lyric ideas.

About a week after this lesson, give students the opportunity to share highlights from their handouts and to discuss their experiences and behavior choices regarding anxiety during the week.

Primary Grade Modifications

BRAINSTORMING STRESS INDICATORS—Give examples, such as first day at school, at home alone with a baby-sitter, going to the doctor. You may want to demonstrate movements for the students.

INQUIRY—Provide examples first.

SELF-TALK—Change the situation about which students are thinking to one in which they imagine that their parents are going out for the night and they will be staying with a new baby-sitter.

SCENE INVESTIGATION—Change the situation to being left with a new sitter and revise the scene as appropriate, using the lesson scene as reference.

REFLECTIVE DETECTIVE—Have students draw a double-sided picture. One side represents anxiety and the other, calmness.

Middle and High School Modifications

BRAINSTORMING STRESS INDICATORS—Use age-appropriate examples, such as going out on a first date, deciding on colleges, an opening night performance, or a big game.

INQUIRY—If students are uncomfortable sharing feelings, these can be written anonymously and read aloud.

SCENE INVESTIGATION—Encourage students to develop their own scenes with the one given as a reference.

UNCOVERING FEELINGS

Sometimes people find it difficult to identify or express their feelings. It may seem at times that people are not supposed to let out their feelings, let those feelings show, cry, or talk about them. People might try to hide their feelings and hope that the feelings will go away. But these feelings do not disappear, they just hide out. These feelings may sometimes make a person ill and may lead to what are known as *psychosomatic diseases*. Also, they may affect choices made without a person being aware that this is happening. An example of this would be when a person is angry with someone but does not deal with the anger immediately. This may lead to getting very angry at someone else in an unrelated situation.

Awareness of feelings enables a person to consciously choose and manage them, figuring out when they are felt, how often they are experienced, and how they are expressed.

Lesson 6 examines beliefs and choices made with regard to covering or uncovering feelings. Activity 1 reinforces and gives practice in cooperation as a life skill. Activity 2 provides additional rehearsal in relaxation skills. Activity 3 provides an opportunity to actively experience masking feelings, whereas Activity 4 offers a chance to examine feelings hidden and feelings shown. Activity 5 builds an awareness of situations in which feelings are covered up. Activity 6 explores the assumption "I must never let out my feelings or it will be awful" through a scene.

Additional ways to encourage expression of feelings are through modeling; sharing your feelings when appropriate and in ways you are comfortable with; encouraging students to share their feelings about events in school as well as in their lives as appropriate; and developing anonymous ways of doing so, such as the use of feelings boxes in which students can write down issues and feelings they wish to talk about, act out, or explore.

Uncovering Feelings

TARGETED EMOTIONAL DOMAINS Self-Awareness, Managing Emotions

TARGETED INTELLIGENCES Verbal/Linguistic, Visual/Spatial, Bodily/Kinesthetic, Intrapersonal, Logical/Mathematical, Naturalist

CURRICULAR AREAS Health, Social Studies, Language Arts, Math, Science

▶ Activity 1: MIRRORS

1. Have the students stand in a circle. Ask one student to be a person looking into a very large mirror. The volunteer slowly moves different parts of his or her body. The remaining students form the mirror and follow the volunteer's movements exactly.

2. Explain that everyone must focus on the volunteer and work together to be a believable mirror. If any one of the mirror students does not follow the movements exactly, it will seem as if there is a crack in the mirror, and the mirror is supposed to be in excellent condition!

3. Discuss with students how the mirror students did. What did they have to do to make the mirror work? What might they have done to make the mirror even more believable? What would have kept the mirror from working well? Was it easy to be the mirror students?

▶ Activity 2: RAGS

Repeat Activity 4 in Lesson 5. For metacognitive discussion, ask students if they experienced sensations that were different than the first time they did this relaxation exercise. What was different this time? What might they do to have the exercise help them relax even more? When might they use this exercise to help them relax?

▶ Activity 3: MASKS

1. Explain that some people want to cover up what they are feeling, so they make sure that their feelings do not show on the outside.

2. Ask students to imagine that they are experiencing one particular feeling. Before the feeling shows, however, they will put an imaginary mask over their

faces and show a different feeling on the outside. Examples that might be used here include

—Imagine that you are feeling sad. Now, put a happy mask over your face so that everyone can see you smiling and no one will know that you are sad.

—Imagine that you are feeling afraid on the inside and would like to scream. Put a show-off mask over your face so that everyone can see that you feel confident and no one will know that you are afraid.

▶ Activity 4: IDEA TREE

Ask students to draw an idea tree with the word *feelings* in the trunk. They are to write the feelings they tend to cover up in the roots and those they show to people in the branches.

▶ Activity 5: INQUIRY

1. Prepare the Feelings Check form by using the four column format (see Blacklines). Write the title at the top of the page. Label the columns *Day, Feeling, Covered,* and *Uncovered.* Add the directions: "Fill in the day and the feeling you felt. Put a check mark under the column labeled 'covered' if you covered up the feeling or under 'uncovered' if you let your feeling out."

2. Ask students to complete the sentence "A time when I kept my feelings inside was . . . ." on the Uncovering Feelings handout (see Blacklines).

3. Introduce the Feelings Check form at the end of the lesson and ask students to fill it out during the week.

▶ Activity 6: SCENE INVESTIGATION: SHARING FEELINGS

1. Tell students that they are going to examine the assumption that

THE ASSUMPTION

> "I must never let out my feelings or it would be awful"

by developing and acting a scene.

2. Develop a scene:

CHOOSE A SITUATION A student receives a poor grade on a test, is sad about it, but smiles to cover up how he or she feels.

ESTABLISH SETTING classroom

IDENTIFY CHARACTERS students and a teacher

PREPARE ROLES TO REFLECT ASSUMPTION

Thoughts

—I'm so upset about this grade.

—I can't believe I did so badly.

—I'd better not let anyone see how I feel though, or they'll think I'm weird.

Feelings

—sad, scared

Behaviors

—The student works hard to keep a smile on his face.

—He gets a headache and stomachache and asks to go to the nurse.

CREATE A STORY LINE AND IDEAS FOR DIALOGUE

A suggested story line begins with the teacher returning a test to the students. "Here are your tests. I know you all did the best you could and will keep working at your top level."

A student, Muneo, who covers up his feelings, looks at his paper and his thoughts are voiced aloud. (This may be done by the student playing the role, or you may want to involve other students who will act as Muneo's "voice.") "I'm so upset about this grade. I can't believe I did so badly. I'd better not let anyone know how I feel, or they'll think I'm weird." The student tries to keep smiling. A classmate asks how he did on the test, and Muneo tries to cover up. "How did you do?" He answers, "Oh, just fine." Muneo tries to keep a smile on his face, but his head begins to hurt and his stomach starts feeling funny. He asks the teacher for permission to go to the nurse. "I'm not feeling very well. May I please be excused?" The teacher answers, "Certainly, Muneo, I hope you feel better."

EXAMPLE STORY LINE "SHARING FEELINGS"

3. Enact the scene: Have students act out the scene. Remind them to use their bodies and voices to show what they are thinking. Try to give each student a chance to share thoughts and feelings. Choose individual students to play the two student parts, and consider using different students to perform the actions and to voice the dialogue.

4. Reflect on the enactment:

THE ASSUMPTION
EXAMINED

EXAMINE ASSUMPTION Remind students that the assumption was "I must never let out my feelings or it would be awful." Students ask three questions:

Am I crystal balling?

Informed choice makers know that it is impossible to predict how it would be if one lets out his or her feelings. There are all kinds of possibilities as to how it would be, but no one can prove that it would be awful.

Am I generalizing?

Informed choice makers know that using the word *must* is an example of exaggerating and that they do have a choice about whether they let out their feelings. The word *never* is also an exaggeration and leaves no room for other possibilities. If a person believes in the assumption, that person may feel that there is no other choice but to cover up his or her feelings. However, if that person examines the assumption, he or she sees that there is another choice—to let out feelings when and how he or she likes.

Am I awfulizing?

Informed choice makers know that it is stretching the truth to believe that something terrible or awful would happen if feelings are let out. It might be somewhat uncomfortable if people believed in the assumption and thus covered up their feelings. However, people might like letting out their feelings more than they like covering them up, and they can see by examining the assumption that nothing terrible would happen if they did.

CHANGE ASSUMPTION The new belief is

THE PROVABLE
BELIEF

> ## "I can let out my feelings."

ACT ON NEW BELIEF Ask students what they can do to help themselves act according to the provable belief.

Feeling

—Observe their bodies and ask themselves what they are feeling, for example, sad.

Thinking

—Observe their thoughts and ask themselves to identify their self-talk, for example, "I feel sad but I must not let anyone know."

Behaving

—Change their self-talk to go along with the provable belief, for example, "I feel sad and it's all right if I let others know how I feel."

Take Action

—They can let someone know how they feel. They can ask for help so they can do better next time.

5. Revise the scene: The same situation, setting, and characters may be used. You may want to use different students in various roles to involve everyone.

PREPARE ROLES TO REFLECT NEW BELIEF

Thoughts

—I'm upset about this grade. Maybe I'd feel better if I let someone know how I feel. It might be difficult at first, but I can make that choice. Maybe I can get help so I can do better next time.

Feelings

—sad, hopeful

Behaviors

—A student allows a frown on his face. He notices that he is upset and tells a friend. He asks his teacher for extra help.

CREATE A STORY LINE AND IDEAS FOR DIALOGUE

The teacher returns a test to the students. "Here are your tests. I know you all did the best you could and will keep working at your top level."

A student, Muneo, receives a bad grade and his thoughts are spoken aloud. "I'm upset about this grade. Maybe I'd feel better if I let someone know how I feel." Muneo realizes that he is unhappy and tells his friend what happened. "I'm really sad because I got a bad grade on the test." His friend answers, "I know how you feel. That makes me sad when I get a bad grade too. Maybe you'll do better next time." The student asks his teacher for some extra help. "I don't think I understood the stuff on the test. Could you help me with it?" The teacher answers, "I would be happy to help you. I'm very proud of you for asking for help."

EXAMPLE STORY LINE "SHARING FEELINGS" REVISED SCENE

6. Students act out the revised scene using their own dialogue and actions.

REFLECTIVE
DETECTIVE   Ask students to research and write a brief lecture, story, or poem on psychosomatic illness.

About a week after the lesson, give students the opportunity to share highlights from their handouts and to discuss their experiences with sharing feelings during the week.

Primary Grade Modifications

IDEA TREE—Do a tree for the students and explain it to them.

INQUIRY—Give some examples first, such as "when I was trying to be brave at the doctor's office."

SCENE INVESTIGATION—Change the situation to that of a student who has moved to a new school and misses his or her old school, friends, and teacher. Revise the scene as appropriate, using the lesson scene as reference.

REFLECTIVE DETECTIVE—Make a two-sided paper plate mask with true feelings showing on one side and with a feeling that everybody would see on the outside on the other side.

Middle and High School Modifications

MIRRORS—Have students do the activity in pairs, trying not to let anyone see who is leading and who is following.

MASKS—Have students choose emotions from their personal experiences. Have them discuss their observations of the effects of masking on body and voice.

SCENE INVESTIGATION—Change the situation to one in which a girl is told that her date for a dance has asked someone else to go with him. Revise the scene as appropriate, using the lesson scene as reference.

All of us become frustrated or angry at times, and for some, this occurs frequently. Various situations trigger anger, and people react in various ways. Some might try to make themselves feel better by hurting themselves or others. Others might keep anger inside and create an illness. Or sometimes, they might keep their feelings inside for a while until they boil over in ways and places they did not intend.

Choosing to become frustrated and angry is based partly on the assumption that "It is awful and I must get angry when things don't go the way I want them to go." This lesson helps students realize that they have a choice of how to react to anger.

Lesson 7 examines beliefs and choices made regarding anger. Activity 1 reinforces cooperation skills. Activity 2 provides a new relaxation method. Activity 3 builds awareness of feelings of anger and sharing strategies that students may use. Activity 4 explores the assumption "It is awful and I must get angry when things don't go the way I want them to go" through a scene.

Additional ways to explore choices around anger include modeling assertiveness and dealing with class situations that elicit anger by discussing choices made, the assumptions upon which they were based, and choosing and rehearsing new options.

DEALING WITH ANGER

Dealing With Anger

LESSON 7

TARGETED EMOTIONAL DOMAINS   Self-Awareness, Managing Emotions, Self-Control, Empathy, Handling Relationships

TARGETED INTELLIGENCES   Verbal/Linguistic, Visual/Spatial, Bodily/Kinesthetic, Logical/Mathematical, Intrapersonal, Interpersonal, Musical/Rhythmic, Naturalist

CURRICULAR AREAS   Health, Social Studies, Language Arts, Math, Science, Music

---

▶ Activity 1: MIRRORS

1. Explain that the students will be creating a mirror as they did in Lesson 6, Activity 1. The person looking into the mirror will move as if he or she is feeling angry. As the mover shows anger through face and body, the rest of the students will mirror him or her exactly.

2. How did the mirror work this time? How was the anger expressed? Are there other ways in which one can express anger? Did they feel any anger as they copied the movements?

▶ Activity 2: SLOW BREATHING

1. Explain that this is another exercise that can be used to help a person relax.

2. Ask students to close their eyes for a moment and to pay attention to the natural rhythm of their breathing. Their breathing is the slowest when they are the most calm and when they are sleeping. As they become more and more anxious or emotional, their breathing becomes more rapid.

3. In order to calm themselves, they can purposely slow their breathing. Ask them to inhale to a slow count of four, using all four counts to take in a full breath. Without holding their breath, they immediately exhale to a slow count of four. (Do this several times.)

4. Ask the students how they feel. Was this exercise different than the rags activity? How do they think they might use this exercise?

▶ Activity 3: INQUIRY

1. Prepare the Anger Check form by using the two column with scale format (see Blacklines). Write the title at the top of the page. Label the columns *Day* and *Amount of Anger*. Add the directions: "Fill in the day and indicate the amount of anger you felt on the scale." Add the word *Anger* to the scale values.

2. Ask students to finish the sentence "A time I got angry was . . . ." on the Anger handout (see Blacklines).

3. Introduce the Anger Check form at the end of the lesson and ask students to fill it out during the week.

▶ Activity 4: SCENE INVESTIGATION: CONTROLLING ANGER

1. Tell students that they are going to examine the assumption

THE ASSUMPTION

> "It is awful and I must get angry when things do not go the way I want them to go."

Create a suitable scene, using the lesson scene as an example.

2. Develop a scene:

   CHOOSE A SITUATION A student attempts to play with a friend while a sibling refuses to stop tagging along.

ESTABLISH SETTING student's bedroom

IDENTIFY CHARACTERS student, friend, sibling, and parents

PREPARE ROLES TO REFLECT ASSUMPTION

Thoughts

—I can't believe she won't leave me alone.

—She is out to make me crazy.

—I hate her.

Feelings

—frustrated, angry

Behaviors

—teasing, yelling, hitting.

CREATE A STORY LINE AND IDEAS FOR DIALOGUE

A student, Megan, and her friend are playing checkers in Megan's bedroom. "This is fun. I like it when you come over." Megan's sister stands at the door and watches. "Can I play too?" Megan's thoughts are voiced. "She's out to make me crazy." She says, "No way, leave us alone." "Why not, I know how to play too," replies the sister. The student thinks, "I hate her," and replies, "Go away. You're a little baby. Play somewhere else." "Please, I promise to be very quiet," says the sister. "I said, get out right now or you're going to regret you're my sister." The sister holds her ground. Megan gets up, goes over to her sister, and pushes her out the door. The sister tries to take a few steps forward, but Megan starts to raise a hand to hit her. At that moment, their mother passes by the bedroom. "I see that you are still having problems getting along with your sister. I'd like you to ask your friend to leave so that we can all sit down and talk and figure out what we can all do to help you get along better."

EXAMPLE STORY LINE
"CONTROLLING ANGER"

3. Enact the scene: Act out the scene with students acting as the characters, the voices, and as active observers who, after the scene, point out nuances of body, voice, and choices made.

4. Reflect on the enactment:

EXAMINE ASSUMPTION Remind students that the assumption was "It is awful and I must get angry when things do not go the way I want them to go." Have them ask the three assumption examining questions that follow.

THE ASSUMPTION
EXAMINED

Am I crystal balling?

Informed choice makers know that it is impossible to predict what will happen if things do not go the way one wants them to go. There are many possibilities about how it might be, but one can not prove that it will be awful.

Am I generalizing?

Informed choice makers know that it is an exaggeration to use the word *must*. There is a choice about how to feel when things do not go the way one wants them to go, even though it may be difficult to make that choice, at first.

Am I awfulizing?

Informed choice makers know that it is stretching the truth to believe that it is awful if things do not go the way one would like. One might prefer things to be different, but one can not prove that it is awful if they are not different than they are.

CHANGE ASSUMPTION The new belief is

THE PROVABLE BELIEF

"Sometimes I would prefer things to be different than they are, but I do not have to get angry if they are not."

ACT ON NEW BELIEF To adjust to the new belief, students consider these:

Feeling

—Observe their bodies and ask themselves what they are feeling, for example, frustrated, angry.

Thinking

—Observe their thoughts and ask themselves to identify their self-talk. Things are not going the way I want them to go. This is awful. I am so angry!

Behaving

—Change their self-talk to go along with the provable belief. Things are not going the way I want them to go. I would prefer if things were different, but it is not awful if they are not. I do not have to get angry.

Take Action

—They can use an exercise to help them relax. They can get rid of whatever feelings remain in safe ways such as hitting a pillow or pounding on clay. They can look for a positive way to change the situation.

5. Revise the scene:

PREPARE ROLES TO REFLECT NEW BELIEF

Thoughts

—I would prefer that my sister let me play with my friend, alone. I know she just wants some company, but my friend and I would rather have some time by ourselves. I don't have to get angry with her. Maybe I can find some way to deal with this.

Feelings

—concern, hope

Behaviors

—deep breathing, reasoning, seeking help

CREATE A STORY LINE AND IDEAS FOR DIALOGUE

> A student, Megan, and her friend are playing checkers in the student's bedroom. "This is fun. I like it when you come over." The student's sister stands at the door and watches. "Can I play too?" Megan's thoughts are voiced. "I would prefer to play alone with my friend." She takes a slow, deep breath so she will be able to answer calmly. "We would like to play by ourselves." "Why? I know how to play too," the sister replies. Megan thinks, "I'm not going to get angry. I'll try to explain myself to her." "Sometimes I like to play with you, but sometimes, like today, I like to play with my friends in private." "I promise to be very quiet," replies the sister. The student thinks, "I don't know what to do. Maybe mom can help."
>
> At that moment, their mother passes by the bedroom. The student says, "Mom, we would like to play by ourselves right now, and she would like to play with us. I tried to get her to understand that, but she won't take no for an answer." Mom replies, "I'm glad you tried to explain yourself to your sister. I'm also proud of you for coming to me for help rather than arguing or fighting. Your sister and I will do something together. Maybe after you two have some time alone, you'll ask her to join you for a while. Is that all right with all of you?" All reply, "Yes."

EXAMPLE STORY LINE "CONTROLLING ANGER" REVISED SCENE

6. Students act out the revised scene.

REFLECTIVE
DETECTIVE
Discuss and demonstrate the boiling point of water, allowing the water to boil over. Then follow this with a pantomime of being "boiling mad," first boiling over and then showing a different way to handle anger.

Also, a week or so following this lesson, at any day or time convenient to you, give students the opportunity to share highlights from their handouts and to discuss a time since the lesson when they felt frustrated or angry and how they dealt with those feelings.

Primary Grade Modifications

SCENE INVESTIGATION—Change the situation to reflect the point of view of the younger sibling wants to play with an older sibling who refuses. Revise the scene to reflect the new situation, using the lesson scene as reference.

REFLECTIVE DETECTIVE—Have students draw or collect pictures of things that make them angry, then tear them up and put them in the garbage.

Middle and High School Modifications

Have students give examples of the different ways they have handled anger, discussing the changes in body, voice, and consequences based on each choice.

MIRRORS—Do a series of mirrors revealing a continuum of anger from slightly perturbed through enraged. Discuss the similarities and differences between each.

SCENE INVESTIGATION—Change the situation to be one in which a teen fights an early curfew. Revise the scene to accommodate the new situation, using the lesson scene as reference.

Many times, people do not know what they are responsible for, what they have directly caused, and what are responsibilities of others. Sometimes they understand that they are responsible for their choices; sometimes they believe that they are not responsible for their own choices; and sometimes they believe that they are responsible for others' choices as well as their own.

It is important to determine one's responsibility based on facts and not assumptions, so that one acknowledges appropriate responsibility but not inappropriate guilt. Two related assumptions serve as the foundation for this assumption: "I am responsible for everything. I am responsible for nothing."

Lesson 8 examines assumptions related to one's degree of responsibility for various choices. Activity 1 encourages active examination of students' assumptions relating to responsibility. Activity 2 builds the students' ability to determine when they are responsible for something. Activity 3 explores the twin assumptions "I am responsible for everything, I am responsible for nothing" through a scene.

Additional ways to encourage the assumption of appropriate responsibility are modeling and discussing choices for which students are responsible, rather than accepting phrases such as "I had no choice."

EXAMINING AND ACCEPTING RESPONSIBILITY

Examining and Accepting Responsibility

LESSON 8

TARGETED EMOTIONAL DOMAINS Self Awareness, Handling Relationships

TARGETED INTELLIGENCES Verbal/Linguistic, Visual/Spatial, Bodily/Kinesthetic, Logical/Mathematical, Naturalist, Intrapersonal, Interpersonal

CURRICULAR AREAS Health, Social Studies, Language Arts, Math, Science

---

▶ Activity 1: RESPONSIBILITY VOTE

1. Tell students that they are going to vote to determine situations in which they would take responsibility and those in which they would not take responsibility. Some people assume that they are not responsible for their own choices. Some people assume that they are responsible for others' choices as well as their own. It is important to examine these assumptions so that a person can determine what is and is not his or her personal responsibility.

2. Explain that you will describe a number of different situations and give the students two choices to vote for: responsible and not responsible. For those situations for which a student would accept responsibility, he or she raises a hand after you say "responsible." Tell them that their answers are to be based on their personal opinions. Examples of situations that might be used include these:

—If your homework is not where you thought you left it, are you responsible for your homework?

—Your den is messy after a friend has been over to play with you. Are you responsible for the mess?

—You said "I wish you were dead" to someone, out of anger, and that person became ill. Are you responsible for their illness?

—Your parents have been fighting, and you overhear your name being mentioned during the fight. Are you responsible for their fighting?

▶ Activity 2: INQUIRY

1. Prepare the Responsibility Check form by using the two column format (see Blacklines). Write the title at the top of the page. Label the columns *Day* and *Situation*. Add the directions: "Fill in the day and the situation. Then, write the word or words that best describe how much of the situation you felt you were responsible for: everything, certain things, nothing."

2. Ask students to complete the inquiry sentence—"A time I felt totally responsible or not responsible was . . . ." on the Responsibility handout (see Blacklines).

3. Introduce the Responsibility Check form at the end of the lesson and ask students to fill it out during the week.

▶ Activity 3: SCENE INVESTIGATION: DETERMINING RESPONSIBILITY

1. Tell students that they are to examine the following assumptions:

THE ASSUMPTION

> "I am responsible for everything.
> I am responsible for nothing."

Create a suitable scene, using the example scene as a starting point.

2. Develop a scene:

CHOOSE A SITUATION a trial

ESTABLISH SETTING a courtroom

IDENTIFY CHARACTERS defendants, judge, and jury members

PREPARE ROLES TO REFLECT ASSUMPTION

Thoughts

Responsible—Everything that happens is my fault. I take full responsibility. Blame me.

Not Responsible—Nothing that happens is my fault. It is not my responsibility. Do not blame me.

Feelings

Responsible—guilt, remorse, sadness

Not responsible—frustration, confusion

Behaviors

Responsible—describing the situation in gory detail, apologizing, asking for punishment

Not responsible—making the situation seem like "no big deal," making excuses, claiming he or she doesn't belong on trial

CREATE A STORY LINE AND IDEAS FOR DIALOGUE

The judge calls the court to order. "The court is now in session. In this first hearing, the defendants will describe their situations with as much detail as possible. They will describe what happened and the part they played in what happened. They will then state whether they feel they are responsible or not responsible. I would like the jury of choice detectives to listen very carefully. In the second session, they will vote as to the responsibility of each defendant. Defendant number one, please describe your situation."

Defendant number one thinks, "I hope I get punished for this because it was all my fault." He then says, "Well, your honor, I was very angry with my mother because she wouldn't let me sleep over at my friend's house. I'm working on not getting angry, but it's still a new thing for me. Well, when I was angry at my mother, I thought to myself, 'I wish you were dead.' My mother has been sick for the past few days and I know it must be because of what I thought. It's my fault that she's sick, I take all the blame. I'm so sorry for making her sick. I'm fully responsible and I must be punished."

The judge calls on the second defendant. "Defendant number two, please describe your situation."

EXAMPLE STORY LINE "DETERMINING RESPONSIBILITY"

> Defendant number two thinks, "I don't really know why I'm here. It's not my fault." She then says, "I guess I'll tell you what happened even though it had nothing to do with me. We were working on a project in class and the teacher had asked us to work in silence. Well, everyone was talking anyway and we got in trouble. I don't know why I'm here, though. Everyone was talking so I had to talk too. If someone asks you something you have to answer them. I had no choice. I had to talk. It's not my fault. Don't blame me because I'm not responsible."
>
> The judge says, "Court will take a brief recess to look at some clues. We will meet again to discuss these cases further."

3. Enact the scene: Have students act out the scene, using their own dialogue and speaking their own thoughts and feelings. It is possible to have one student do the acting and another student be the voice that speaks the dialogue. It is also useful to have observers.

4. Reflect on the enactment:

THE ASSUMPTION
EXAMINED

EXAMINE ASSUMPTION Remind students that the assumptions were "I am responsible for everything. I am responsible for nothing." Students ask the one assumption examining question that applies (Am I crystal balling? and Am I awfulizing? do not apply in this case):

Am I generalizing?

Informed choice makers know that using the words *everything* and *nothing* are examples of exaggeration. It is not possible that one could be responsible for every single thing that happens. It is not possible that one could be responsible for absolutely nothing that happens. There is a possibility that one might be responsible for some things. A person can look at the facts in order to determine his or her responsibility.

CHANGE ASSUMPTION The new belief is

THE PROVABLE
BELIEF

> "There are certain things for which I am responsible and certain things for which I am not responsible."

ACT ON NEW BELIEF Ask students to suggest ways that they could behave or feel that would support the provable belief.

Feeling

—Observe their bodies and ask themselves what they are feeling.

Responsible—guilt, remorse, sadness

Not responsible—frustration, confusion

Thinking

—Observe their thoughts and ask themselves to identify their self-talk.

Responsible—Something happened and it is totally my fault. I must be punished.

Not responsible—Something happened but it has nothing to do with me. I should not be blamed.

Behaving

—Change their self-talk to go along with the provable belief.

Responsible—Something happened for which I may or may not be responsible. I can examine the facts.

Not responsible—Something happened for which I may or may not be responsible. I can examine the facts.

Take Action

—Examine the facts to determine where the responsibility rests. Students ask themselves the following questions: Did the situation arise as a direct result of what I did? Was the situation a result of my choice even though I may have made the same choice many others made or was the situation a result of someone else's choice? If I determine that I am responsible, I can take whatever action is possible to remedy the situation, and then relax and let it go. If I determine that I am not responsible, I can accept that there is nothing I can do, allow whoever is responsible to make their own choice to remedy the situation, then relax and let it go.

5. Revise the scene:

PREPARE ROLES TO REFLECT NEW BELIEF

Thoughts

—Some things that happen are my responsibility. I can examine the facts and then act accordingly.

Feelings

—acceptance, satisfaction

Behaviors

—explaining the situation as it happened with little exaggeration, accepting responsibility as the facts dictate, taking action or letting others take action

CREATE A STORY LINE AND IDEAS FOR DIALOGUE

EXAMPLE STORY LINE
"DETERMINING
RESPONSIBILITY"
REVISED SCENE

The judge calls the court back to order. "The court is now in session to determine the responsibility of the defendants. First, the jury of choice detectives will give their verdict as to the responsibility of each defendant. Then defendants will restate their cases based on the provable belief that we examined and state again whether they feel they are responsible or not responsible."

The jury votes on the responsibility of each defendant. (This can be done by a show of hands or secret ballot.)

Defendant number one thinks, "I don't believe that this was my fault. My mother's sickness was not in my control." He says, "Your honor, I was very angry at my mother because she wouldn't let me sleep at a friend's house. When I was angry, I thought to myself, 'I wish you were dead.' My mother has been sick the past few days, but I know I am not at fault for that. I do not have the power to make her sick. Her illness is not a direct result of what I thought. I would like her to feel better, but I can't help her to feel better by wrongly thinking that I am to blame. All I can do is help her any way that I can and let go of blaming myself. Your honor, I am not responsible for my mother's illness."

Defendant number two thinks, "I believe that this is my fault. Even though others were talking, I made my own choice to talk." She says, "Your honor, we were working on a project in class and the teacher had asked us to work in silence. Well, everyone was talking anyway, and we got in trouble. Even though everyone else was talking, I made my own choice to talk. It might have been difficult to stay quiet while others were talking, but I could have. Next time the situation comes up, I will remember that I have a choice to make. Your honor, I am responsible for talking in class."

6. Have students reenact the scene using new dialogue that expresses their feelings and behavior after examining and changing the assumption.

REFLECTIVE
DETECTIVE

Design and demonstrate an example of cause and effect.

Also, a week or so after this lesson, give students the opportunity to share highlights from their handouts and to discuss a time during the week following the lesson when they felt wrongly accused or when they felt completely responsible and how they dealt with those feelings. They may read from their Responsibility

Check handouts or talk about their week. No one comments unless students who share would like comments or ask for suggestions.

Primary Grade Modifications

RESPONSIBILITY VOTE—Define responsibility as something that the individual made happen. You may want to delete the homework example.

SCENE INVESTIGATION—Change the situation so defendant one is angry because his mother was unwilling to buy him a new toy; defendant two's situation was that she would not stop running around the room when the teacher asked her to stop. Revise the scene to accommodate this new situation, using the lesson scene as reference.

REFLECTIVE DETECTIVE—Ask students to draw pictures of themselves holding up all the things for which they are responsible.

Middle and High School Modifications

RESPONSIBILITY VOTE—Use additional examples, such as Are you responsible for your basic body type? Are you responsible for keeping a secret if revealing that secret could protect someone? Also, brainstorm the excuses used for shirking responsibility.

SCENE INVESTIGATION—Change defendant one's situation to reflect that he was angry with his mother because his mother insisted that he return home after a party by 11:00 p.m. Change the situation for defendant two to that of drinking at a party.

CHOOSING HAPPINESS

Feeling happy, like all other feelings, is based on a choice that one makes. A person can be happy at any moment if that person chooses to be. Often, people believe that something outside of themselves brings them happiness. Some may hold off being happy until everything in their lives is exactly as they want, believing that will bring them happiness. Some may choose to wait until people act toward them the way they would want them to before they allow themselves to be happy. Or, others may choose to wait until they possess all they would want, such as toys, popularity, or clothes, before they choose to feel happy.

Lesson 9 looks at choices made with regard to happiness. Activity 1 builds students' awareness of the ability to choose happiness in their daily activities. Activity 2 explores the effects of happiness on body and voice, giving students the opportunity to identify the characteristic body language of happiness. Activity 3 provides experience in the use of guided fantasy to enhance emotions. Activity 4 provides an opportunity to brainstorm and diagram positive and negative methods of enhancing happiness. Activity 5 explores the assumption "I can never be happy, and life will be awful unless certain things are a certain way" through a scene.

Additional ways to encourage the choice of happiness are modeling, sharing realistic ways of dealing with sadness while not staying in that emotional place, and encouraging students to focus on positive thoughts and behaviors.

LESSON 9

Choosing Happiness

TARGETED EMOTIONAL DOMAINS   Self-Awareness, Managing Emotions, Self-Control

TARGETED INTELLIGENCES   Verbal/Linguistic, Visual/Spatial, Logical/Mathematical, Bodily/Kinesthetic, Musical/Rhythmic, Intrapersonal, Naturalist

CURRICULAR AREAS   Language Arts, Health, Social Studies, Math, Music, Science

---

▶ Activity 1: INQUIRY

1. Prepare the Happiness Check form by using the three column format (see Blacklines). Write the title at the top of the page. Label the columns *Day, Unhappy,* and *Happy*. Add the directions: "Fill in the day and mark 'Unhappy' if you were unhappy that day or 'Happy' if you were happy that day."

2. Ask students to complete the inquiry sentence—"A time when I felt unhappy was . . . ." on the Happiness handout (see Blacklines).

3. Introduce the Happiness Check form at the end of the lesson and ask students to fill it out during the week.

▶ Activity 2: MOVING SCULPTURE

1. Explain that everyone in the class is to combine wordlessly to create a sculpture that would express happiness through their collective bodies.

2. After the sculpture is formed and on the count of three, the sculpture moves in a way that would express happiness.

3. On the next count of three, students add to the sculpture sounds, words, or melodies that would express happiness through their voices.

4. Ask students how the sculpture formed. What made it more or less difficult to do this? How were decisions made about movement? What were the pictures, movement, and sound qualities that expressed happiness?

▶ Activity 3: GUIDED FANTASY

1. Explain to students that when people daydream, they are able to see all kinds of pictures in their minds.

2. Tell students that you are going to help them to see a particular kind of picture in their minds, right now. Ask them to close their eyes and listen to the sound of your voice. Reassure them that because everyone's eyes are closed and there will be nothing to see, they can feel comfortable about keeping their eyes shut. As they listen to the sound of your voice, ask them to picture in their minds what you are describing.

3. Tell students that right now they are sitting in chairs in a classroom. Ask them to imagine that their chair and the classroom have disappeared and that they are now sitting on the grass in the middle of a huge field. Tell them to feel the softness of the grass beneath them. This grass is allergy free, so there is no need to be concerned about health problems.

4. Ask them, in their minds, to look around them. It is a beautiful place, filled with all the things that they find beautiful. Tell them to look in front of them and see what is there; to listen carefully to the sounds around them; to hear all their favorite sounds; to breathe deeply; and to smell all the wonderful fragrances that surround them.

5. Explain that this is a safe place, a place where they are always happy. They can be alone here, or they can bring people they like with them. In their minds,

they are to see themselves doing all the things that they enjoy in this special place and to pay attention to all the positive happy thoughts they have here.

6. Tell them that they are going to leave this place in a few moments. However, this is a place that they can come back to on their own. In their minds, they say good-bye to this special place for now, knowing that they can return.

7. Ask them to pay attention to the feeling of their chair underneath them and the sounds and smells of the classroom and to slowly open their eyes.

▶ Activity 4: BRAINSTORMING A VENN DIAGRAM

1. This activity requires that students know about Venn diagrams.

2. Explain that the students are to brainstorm as many positive ways of becoming happier as they can. Then, they brainstorm as many negative ways of becoming happier as they can. Discuss with them that *positive ways* would be ways that do not harm themselves or others and do not go against the law or their beliefs. *Negative ways* would include ways that are harmful to themselves or others and are against the law or their beliefs.

3. Have them create a Venn diagram to illustrate their findings. Examples of ways of becoming happier might include the following:

—Positive

thinking positive, happy thoughts by counting our blessings

doing something we like to do

taking ourselves to our special place

helping another person to feel happier

—Negative

acting out

trying to make someone else feel bad

doing something to excess, such as staying in a fantasy world, spending a lot of money, or overeating

stealing

taking a drink

▶ Activity 5: SCENE INVESTIGATION: CHOOSING HAPPINESS

1. Explain to students that they are to develop and act in a scene to examine this assumption about happiness:

> "I can never be happy, and life will be awful
> unless certain things are a certain way."

THE ASSUMPTION

Create a suitable scene, using the example as a reference.

2. Develop a scene:

CHOOSE A SITUATION a "Happiness Talk Show" where guests talk about how they thought they could never be happy and then learned to be happy

ESTABLISH SETTING a talk show set

IDENTIFY CHARACTERS host, guests, and audience members

PREPARE ROLES TO REFLECT ASSUMPTION

Thoughts

—Everything is not the way I want and therefore I cannot be happy. I need something to make me happy.

Feelings

—frustration, unhappiness

Behaviors

—involvement in activities that do not make them happy

—blaming their unhappiness on everything other than themselves

—getting into trouble

CREATE A STORY LINE AND IDEAS FOR DIALOGUE

The host welcomes the guests to the show and invites them to share their experiences. "Welcome to the Happiness Show, where we find how unhappiness can turn into happiness by each person's choice. First, we would like our guests to tell us how they believed they would find happiness. Then, each guest describes or demonstrates what you did to find it, what happened, and how you found out that this was not the path to your happiness. Would you care to share your experiences with us?" (Allow several students to pick a negative method of finding happiness and share their experiences. One example is shown here.)

A guest, Bill, shares his experiences. "Well, I believed that the only way I could be happy was if I had all the toys I wanted, particularly the new ones they showed on television. I would think, 'As soon as I get that new Ninja Turtle, that will make me the happiest person alive.' So I would nag and nag my parents until they couldn't stand it any more. I would cry and say things like, 'If you really

EXAMPLE STORY LINE
"CHOOSING HAPPINESS"

> loved me, you'd want me to be happy and you'd buy it for me.' They finally got me what I wanted, I looked at it for a few minutes and had fun, but then I put it away and didn't look at it again. I thought it would make me happy, but it really didn't."

3. Enact the scene: Have students act out the scene, creating their own dialogue and actions as they do.

4. Reflect on the enactment:

THE ASSUMPTION
EXAMINED

EXAMINE ASSUMPTION Remind students that the assumption is "I can never be happy, and life will be awful unless certain things are a certain way." Students ask three questions to examine the assumption:

Am I crystal balling?

Informed choice makers know that it is not possible to predict one's happiness in the future. Even if certain things were a certain way, it would not be possible to know how one would feel then.

Am I generalizing?

Informed choice makers know that it is exaggerating to use the word *never*. One might prefer if certain things were a certain way. However, it is stretching the truth to say that one could never be happy if things are not the way one would like them to be.

Am I awfulizing?

Informed choice makers know that it is stretching the truth to believe that life would be awful if things were not the way they would like them to be. One might prefer that things were a certain way, but one cannot prove that life would be awful, were they not.

CHANGE ASSUMPTION The new belief is

THE PROVABLE
BELIEF

> "I can be happy if I choose to be happy."

ACT ON NEW BELIEF Students consider the following as a means of reflecting the new belief:

Feeling

—Observe their bodies and ask themselves what they are feeling, for example, frustration, unhappiness.

Thinking

—Observe their thoughts and ask themselves to identify their self-talk. For example, "Certain things are not the way I would like them to be, therefore I cannot be happy."

Behaving

—Change their self-talk to go along with the provable belief. For example, "I would prefer certain things to be different than they are. However, that cannot stop me from being happy if I choose to be happy."

Take Action

—Think positive thoughts, do something positive.

5. Revise the scene:

PREPARE ROLES TO REFLECT NEW BELIEF

Thoughts

—I can be happy even if things aren't exactly the way I want them to be. It's my choice.

Feelings

—relief, happiness

Behaviors

—thinking about the things that are going well, acknowledging but not becoming upset about those that are not, imagining their "happy place," doing enjoyable activities

CREATE A STORY LINE AND IDEAS FOR DIALOGUE

The host welcomes everyone back to the show. "Hello again and welcome back to the Happiness Show. Now we will find out how each guest was able to choose happiness. Guests may describe how their beliefs changed, describe or demonstrate what they did differently, and tell how they found happiness. Would you please tell us about your experiences?" (Allow several students to share a positive method of finding happiness. I provide one example here.)

A guest, Leilani, shares her experiences. "I knew that there were some things in my life that I would have preferred to be different. There were some things I wanted that I didn't have. I would have liked to be better at certain things like math and spelling. However, those things did not determine my happiness, I did. I knew that I could choose to feel good or choose to focus on the things I wanted to be different. I worked at improving my math and my spelling but

EXAMPLE STORY LINE "CHOOSING HAPPINESS" REVISED SCENE

> I did not become upset that I was not farther along than I was. I decided to feel happy about the things in my life that I enjoyed, and to do some other positive things like swimming and riding my bike. When I forget that I can choose to be happy, I sometimes imagine that I'm in my special place, and being there reminds me that I can be happy when I choose to be happy."

6. Have students act out the revised scene, supplying dialogue and gestures as they think appropriate.

REFLECTIVE DETECTIVE

Create a scientific formula for happiness.

Also, a week or so after this lesson, give students the opportunity to share highlights from their handouts and to discuss a time in the week following the lesson when they felt happiest and how they arrived at that feeling. They may read from their Happiness Check handouts or talk about their week. No one comments unless students who share would like comments or ask for suggestions.

Primary Grade Modifications

MOVING SCULPTURE—Be more directive, using ideas from the students.

BRAINSTORMING A VENN DIAGRAM—Do the brainstorming but eliminate the Venn diagram unless students are reading. In this case, do the diagram for them.

SCENE INVESTIGATION—Consider changing the situation in the revised scene to replace math and spelling with art and sports.

REFLECTIVE DETECTIVE—Have each student draw their happy place and describe it to the rest of the class.

Middle and High School Modifications

MOVING SCULPTURE—Discuss the specific ways happiness is expressed in bodies and voices on a day-to-day basis. Also, talk about how one allows oneself to express happiness in different ways as one gets older.

GUIDED FANTASY—Have students draw a picture of their special place.

BRAINSTORMING A VENN DIAGRAM—Discuss personal, peer, and societal pressures to engage in negative methods of enhancing happiness.

SCENE INVESTIGATION—Change the situation so that the guest believed that if she had all the friends she wanted, she would be popular and happy.

PART II

Choosing to
THINK WISELY

CHAPTER 3

Developing Emotional Intelligence Through

SELF-CONCEPT AND RELATIONSHIPS

A critical feature of informed decision making is for the chooser to clearly perceive his or her own abilities. This chapter focuses on students' acceptance of themselves, a pervasive ingredient of one's intrapersonal intelligence. Accepting oneself, including one's mistakes, is a skill that, for many, requires attention and careful development.

The first three lessons in this chapter introduce students to the ideas of self-worth and self-measurement. Students examine their concepts of themselves, consider different methods of evaluating their self-worth, and investigate the concept of perfectionism as an emotional pitfall in intrapersonal intelligence.

In the final two lessons, students apply their informed choice-making understanding to relationships. Students examine how they behave toward friends and family and consider how they may choose behaviors to improve their friendships and relations with family members.

SkyLight Training and Publishing Inc.

DEVELOPING SELF-ACCEPTANCE

People may choose whether to accept themselves for who they are. This choice is based on a number of assumptions that can be discovered if they learn to pay attention to the statements they tell themselves about themselves—their *self-talk* that plays inside their minds like an ongoing tape.

Some people make up their own statements, but sometimes their self-talk statements are comments that others, such as peers, teachers, and family members, have made first. A person often believes these statements without checking whether they are true, assuming that if others say them, they must be true. Then, the person begins to rehearse those same statements, arriving at his or her self-talk independently. But still, the self-talk is not necessarily based on fact.

When people believe their self-talk, they help or hurt themselves depending on the nature of their self-conversation—whether positive or negative. Self-talk can be a large factor in someone's level of self-esteem. It is worthwhile to examine these statements and explore self-talk that can help a person feel good about him- or herself.

Lesson 10 helps students examine their self-talk and explore nurturing ways they can talk to themselves. Activity 1 provides additional practice in cooperation. Activity 2 gives students another stress management technique. Activity 3 offers an exploration of students' levels of self-acceptance. Activity 4 builds students' positive self-talk skills. Activity 5 helps students identify and share both negative and positive self-talk.

Additional ways to encourage self-acceptance are to model positive self-talk, sharing good things about yourself as well as listening to students' self-talk; to discourage focus on negativity and weakness; and to encourage focus on positive comments and building on strengths.

LESSON 10

Developing Self-Acceptance

TARGETED EMOTIONAL DOMAINS   Self-Awareness, Managing Emotions

TARGETED INTELLIGENCES   Verbal/Linguistic, Visual/Spatial, Logical/Mathematical, Bodily/Kinesthetic, Intrapersonal, Naturalist

CURRICULAR AREAS   Health, Language Arts, Social Studies, Math, Science

---

▶ Activity 1: WORDS

1. Tell students that they are to create a word by forming each letter of the word. (This activity is similar to Alphabet, Lesson 2, Activity 1.)

---

2. Give the students a word to form. For metacognitive discussion, ask students if the letters in the word were easier or harder to form than they were the first time they formed letters. Ask them what they think is different about how they are working together now.

▶ Activity 2: RAGS

Do the relaxation exercise as described in Lesson 5, Activity 5. Ask students if they use this activity to relax. How have they used this or other relaxation activities in their lives?

▶ Activity 3: SELF-ACCEPTANCE BAROMETER

1. Clear space for the students to stand between beginning and end points, which you designate. Use the examples provided or create your own opinions for the barometer.

2. Explain that the students are going to create a barometer to measure a number of different opinions. This barometer is simple: It consists of (1) an imaginary line between the beginning and end points that you point out and (2) the students as actual points on the line. Designate one end of the barometer as high, the other as low, and mark the quarter points, perhaps by using a local landmark along the line, to help students find their way to an appropriate degree between high and low. Remind them that a weather barometer measures different degrees of pressure and explain that this opinion barometer measures different degrees of opinion.

3. Explain to the students that you will make a statement, and they are to share their opinion on the statement by taking a position on the opinion barometer that represents their degree of feeling about the statement. After a moment to decide how they feel about what you say, they stand on the part of the barometer that reflects their opinion. Assure them that there is no right or wrong answer, so they are to take a stand based on their own personal opinion. Even if their friend or every other student is on a different part of the barometer, encourage them to stay with what they feel. Examples of statements you might make include

   —"I feel good about myself." Stand on the line according to how much of the time you feel this way, for example, 0% of the time, 25% of the time, 50% of the time, 100% of the time.

   —"I like myself." Stand on the line according to the degree to which you like yourself, that is, not at all, a little bit, quite a bit, a great deal.

METACOGNITIVE
DISCUSSION Construct a barometer that reflects the full range of self-acceptance. Then give a "self-acceptance report" like a weather report, stating the "self-acceptance readings" like barometric pressure readings.

▶ Activity 4: INQUIRY

Ask students to complete the positive sentences on the Self-Acceptance handout (see Blacklines).

▶ Activity 5: TUNING IN TO SELF-TAPES

1. Explain that in this activity students are going to tune in to the statements they think about themselves.

2. Ask them to spend a moment thinking about all the negative statements they tell themselves, then write these statements on a separate page in their journal. For example, a student might think

   —I'm stupid.

   —I can never do anything right.

   —Nobody likes me.

3. The things people tell themselves about themselves can make them feel bad—or good. It is important for people to examine these things to see if they are true and to work toward telling themselves positive things so they can feel good more often. Ask students to spend a moment thinking about all the positive sentences they tell themselves or that they could tell themselves. Then, ask them to write them on a new page in their journals. Examples of positive thoughts that students might record include

   —I'm nice.

   —I do well in math.

   —I'm a good friend.

4. Go around the room and have each student read at least one positive statement he or she wrote about him- or herself. If a student has a difficult time thinking of positive statements, have the student ask a classmate to offer a suggestion.

REFLECTIVE
DETECTIVE Ask students to examine the assumptions in the statements they wrote for both the negative and positive thoughts. Is there a difference in the assumptions, for

example, are there more provable beliefs in the positive or negative statements? Does the negative thought seem as real when it is written out as when they heard it in their head? Then, ask them to tear out that page of negative thoughts from their journal, crumple it up, and throw it in the wastebasket.

A week or so after this lesson, give students the opportunity to share positive statements from their handouts and to discuss statements from their self-tapes that they were aware of during the week.

Primary Grade Modifications

WORDS—Create a series of connected shapes if letters are too difficult.

SELF-ACCEPTANCE BAROMETER—Demonstrate first.

TUNING INTO SELF-TAPES—Instead of using *negative,* use *bad* and give examples first. Then, change the word *positive* to *good* and give examples first.

REFLECTIVE DETECTIVE—Ask students to draw a life-sized picture of themselves and fill the drawing with pictures or magazine clippings representing all their best qualities.

Middle and High School Modifications

SELF-ACCEPTANCE BAROMETER—Have students provide the items for the barometer.

TUNING INTO SELF-TAPES—Include others' negative and positive comments as well.

EXAMINING SELF-MEASURE-MENT

Some people choose not to accept themselves if they do not measure up to the standards they set for themselves. Often, they use others as their standard of measurement, and they choose not to accept themselves unless they are as talented, intelligent, good-looking, rich, athletic, or any number of other characteristics as someone else. Sometimes they do not realize that they are unable to change or do not control many of their characteristics. Some characteristics are determined by genes, opportunities that occur, and other factors over which individuals have no choice. In addition, these may not be the most important characteristics with which to measure worth.

Lesson 11 examines assumptions and choices made regarding the criteria that may be used to measure self-worth. Activity 1 explores the characteristics for which people have choices and those they do not. Activity 2 builds students' awareness of their self-measurement behavior. Activity 3 explores the assumption "It is awful and I must not accept myself until I measure up to everyone else" through a scene.

Additional ways to encourage self-acceptance without comparison to others are modeling, providing activities where students work toward their own personal bests, and discouraging comparative comments.

LESSON 11

Examining Self-Measurement

TARGETED EMOTIONAL DOMAINS   Self-Awareness, Managing Emotions

TARGETED INTELLIGENCES   Verbal/Linguistic, Visual/Spatial, Logical/Mathematical, Bodily/Kinesthetic, Intrapersonal, Naturalist

CURRICULAR AREAS   Health, Social Studies, Language Arts, Math, Science

▶ Activity 1: CHOICE/NO CHOICE

1. Explain that there are some personal characteristics that a person can change and others that he or she cannot change.

2. In this activity, list a series of characteristics and tell students that, as they consider each characteristic individually, they are to raise their hand when you say *choice* if they believe that they can change that characteristic. Otherwise they raise their hand when you say *no choice* to show that they believe

that they cannot change that characteristic. Examples of characteristics include

—height

—weight

—color of skin

—how we express our feelings

—the year we were born

—how we handle anxiety

—the size of our families

—the color of our eyes

—the way our bodies are built

▶ Activity 2: INQUIRY

1. Prepare the Measuring Check form by using the three column format (see Blacklines). Write the title at the top of the page. Label the columns *Day, Measured,* and *Accepted.* Add the directions: "Fill in the day and check under 'Measured' if you measured yourself against someone else or under 'Accepted' if you accepted yourself without measuring."

2. Ask students to complete the inquiry sentence—"I sometimes feel bad about myself because, compared to everyone else, I . . . ." on the Self-Measurement handout (see Blacklines).

3. Introduce the Measuring Check form and ask students to fill it out during the week.

▶ Activity 3: SCENE INVESTIGATION: SELF-THOUGHTS

1. Tell students that the assumption to be examined in this scene is

THE ASSUMPTION

> "It is awful and I must not accept myself until I measure up to everyone else."

Create a suitable scene, using the lesson scene as an example or starting point.

2. Develop a scene:

CHOOSE A SITUATION a letter to a secret pen pal about feelings about not doing well in gym class

ESTABLISH SETTING a gym

IDENTIFY CHARACTERS the pen pal, the letter writer/reader, measuring student, gym teacher, and fellow classmates

PREPARE ROLES TO REFLECT ASSUMPTION

Thoughts

—It's awful because I'm not as good in gym as everybody else.

—I stink.

Feelings

—frustration, embarrassment, anger

Behaviors

—negative self-talk

—making excuses to get out of gym

—trying to avoid all sports

CREATE A STORY LINE AND IDEAS FOR DIALOGUE

EXAMPLE STORY LINE
"SELF-THOUGHT"

The letter writer reads his or her letter aloud while the pen pal listens, and the others act out the events being described.

Dear Pen Pal, I am writing to tell you about how awful it is in gym class. I walk into the gym and the teacher says "We're going to warm up by running a few laps around the gym." That's where the problems begin. I never could run very fast so I'm always way behind everyone else. Then the teacher says "All right, class. We're going to practice shooting basketballs." Now right away I think "There is no way that I will ever get the ball to go into that hoop. Almost everyone here is taller than I am and everyone is definitely better than I am." That's when I tell the teacher "I'm really not feeling very well. I'd like to sit off to the side for a while." That's how it is with all sports. I'm just no good, so I sit and watch.

3. Enact the scene: Have students act out the scene, using their own dialogue and actions.

4. Reflect on the enactment:

THE ASSUMPTION
EXAMINED

EXAMINE ASSUMPTION Remind students that the assumption was "It is awful and I must not accept myself until I measure up to everyone else." Have them ask the three assumption examining questions:

Am I crystal balling?

Informed choice makers know that it is impossible to predict whether or not one will ever measure up to everyone else. They also know that it is difficult to base one's acceptance of oneself on something that may or may not happen in the future.

Am I generalizing?

Informed choice makers know that using the words *must* and *everyone* are examples of generalizing. Although they might prefer to measure up, they are exaggerating when they say that they must not accept themselves if they do not measure up. They can choose to accept themselves just because they are who they are. Although they may want to measure up to others, it is an exaggeration to say that they have to measure up to every single person.

Am I awfulizing?

Informed choice makers know that it is stretching the truth to believe that it is awful if one does not measure up. They might prefer to measure up to others, but they cannot prove that it is awful if they do not.

CHANGE ASSUMPTION Students develop a provable belief:

> "I can accept myself without having to measure up to anyone else."

THE PROVABLE BELIEF

ACT ON NEW BELIEF Ask students how they might help themselves to behave according to the new belief.

Feeling

—Observe their bodies and ask themselves what they are feeling, such as frustration, embarrassment, anger.

Thinking

—Observe their thoughts and identify their self-talk, particularly the negative thoughts. I'm not as good in gym as anyone else. I don't like gym and I don't like myself.

Behaving

—Change their self-talk to go along with the provable belief. I would prefer to be as good at gym as everybody else but that may not happen, and that is O.K. My skills in gym may have to do with things over which I have no control such as the way my body is built. I can still accept myself and maybe even enjoy some of the things we do in gym, if I do what I can do.

Take Action

—They can repeat their positive self-talk.

—They can set realistic goals for themselves, trying to improve their skills when they can and accepting their limitations.

5. Revise the scene:

PREPARE ROLES TO REFLECT NEW BELIEF

Thoughts

—I can accept what I can do in gym and improve where I can. I can enjoy myself where I am.

Feelings

—acceptance, relief, joy

Behaviors

—Pen pal gives his or her advice and describes the gym class the way it might be if the advice were followed.

CREATE A STORY LINE AND IDEAS FOR DIALOGUE

EXAMPLE STORY LINE
"SELF-THOUGHTS"
REVISED SCENE

Pen pal says, *If you were to change your assumption to a provable belief, think thoughts, feel feelings, and take action based on that belief, gym class might not turn out to be such a bad time for you. You might begin by believing that it is possible to accept yourself without having to measure up to anyone else. If you believed this, you could go into the class feeling less nervous.*

The teacher might say, "Let's warm up by running a few laps." You might think, "Well, I may not be able to run as fast as others, but I think I'll try to see how fast I can run today and see if I can run a little faster than I did yesterday." You might get so absorbed in running that you wouldn't even notice how fast anyone else was running. When the teacher announced, "Let's practice shooting hoops," you could say to yourself, "I know that the hoop is pretty high for me and I could chicken out and sit on the side. That doesn't sound like much fun. I think I'll try and see just how high I can get the ball to go, even if it never goes in the basket. I might stop worrying about how good I am and start enjoying sports just for the fun of it!"

6. Reenact the scene with the new belief. Students use their own dialogue, gestures, actions, and voices to show what they are thinking and how they are feeling.

Have students draw a suitcase and fill it with all the qualities they possess that will help them survive in the world.

About one week after this lesson, give students the opportunity to share highlights from their handouts and to discuss experiences that they had with self-measurement during the week.

REFLECTIVE DETECTIVE

Primary Grade Modifications

CHOICE/NO CHOICE—After their guesses, make sure students understand what things can be changed and why.

SCENE INVESTIGATION—Replace basketball with somersaults.

Middle and High School Modifications

CHOICE/NO CHOICE—Talk about the time that people spend trying to change things over which they have no choice, such as their looks.

CONSIDERING PERFECTIONISM

Some people refuse to be happy unless and until everything they do is perfect. Sometimes they have a difficult time dealing with limitations and accepting the necessity of making mistakes in order to learn.

Rather than looking at a mistake as a positive opportunity to learn about what they need to do differently, they sometimes look at mistakes as evidence of their failure. This can lead to great anxiety, frustration, and avoidance of trying for fear of failing.

Lesson 12 examines assumptions and choices around the perceived need to be perfect. Activity 1 offers an exercise designed to help students increase their ability to manage stress and anxiety. Activity 2 elicits students' experiences with perfectionism and builds their skill in accepting themselves as something less than perfect. Activity 3 explores the assumption "If I am not always perfect, it is awful" through a scene.

Additional ways to promote this belief are modeling, that is, being honest and openly accepting your own imperfections; tolerance of students' mistakes; praising all worthwhile attempts; and listening for and correcting language that supports perfectionism.

LESSON 12

Considering Perfectionism

TARGETED EMOTIONAL DOMAINS   Self-Awareness, Managing Emotions

TARGETED INTELLIGENCES   Verbal/Linguistic, Visual/Spatial, Logical/Mathematical, Bodily/Kinesthetic, Intrapersonal, Musical/Rhythmic

CURRICULAR AREAS   Health, Social Studies, Language Arts, Math, Music

▶ Activity 1: TENSE/RELAX

1. Explain that the students will learn a new relaxation exercise.

2. Tell students to tense and relax their bodies, one muscle group at a time. Starting at the top of their heads and moving down to their toes, they are to tighten their muscles for a few seconds, so that they are as tense as they can possibly be. Then, they are to relax those muscles completely, letting go of every last bit of the tension, so that there is no tension left.

Ask if this exercise helped them to relax. How is this similar to or different from other exercises they have done? In what situations might they use this exercise?

METACOGNITIVE
DISCUSSION

▶ Activity 2: INQUIRY

1. Prepare the Perfection Check form by using the three column format (see Blacklines). Write the title at the top of the page. Label columns *Day, Perfect,* and *Learned*. Add the directions: "Fill in the day, then check under 'Perfect' if you felt you had to be perfect that day or under 'Learned' if you learned from your mistakes."

2. Ask students to complete this sentence—"A time I felt that I had to be perfect was . . . ." on the Perfectionism handout (see Blacklines).

3. Introduce the Perfection Check form and ask students to fill it out during the week.

▶ Activity 3: SCENE INVESTIGATION: PERFECT OR NOT?

1. Explain that this scene investigates the assumption

> "If I am not always perfect, it is awful."

THE ASSUMPTION

Create a suitable scene, using the scene here as an example.

2. Develop a scene:

CHOOSE A SITUATION trying to complete an in-class assignment perfectly

ESTABLISH SETTING the classroom

IDENTIFY CHARACTERS a student who wants to be perfect, classmates, and a teacher

PREPARE ROLES TO REFLECT ASSUMPTION

Thoughts

—I've made a mistake and that's awful! I must be perfect all the time. I'm a failure.

Feelings

—despair, hopelessness, inadequacy, nervousness

Behaviors

—heavy sighing, fidgeting with pencil and paper, crumpling paper up

CREATE A STORY LINE AND IDEAS FOR DIALOGUE

EXAMPLE STORY LINE
"PERFECT OR NOT?"

The teacher hands out an in-class assignment to be completed within fifteen minutes. "Class, here is your assignment. I'd like you to complete it by the time we leave for recess."

As the assignment is handed out, we hear the thoughts of a student, Marv, who wants to be perfect. "Oh no, that's not enough time to get the assignment to be exactly the way I want it to be. It's going to be awful." As Marv attempts to complete the assignment, he sighs often, fidgets with the pencil and paper, and looks very distressed. He then makes a mistake on the assignment and thinks, "I can't hand this paper in with a mistake. An eraser mark will ruin the whole thing. Just forget it. I'm a failure again." Marv then crumples up the paper and throws it in the garbage can.

The teacher then says, "Time is up. Please hand in your assignments." When the student has nothing to turn in, both teacher and student are disappointed.

3. Enact the scene: Students act out the scene, using their own thoughts, dialogue, and behaviors.

4. Reflect on the enactment:

THE ASSUMPTION
EXAMINED

EXAMINE ASSUMPTION Remind students that the assumption was "If I am not always perfect, it is awful." Students ask the three questions that examine assumptions:

Am I crystal balling?

Informed choice makers know that it is impossible to predict whether one will be perfect in the future. A person might be perfect or imperfect.

Am I generalizing?

Informed choice makers know that using the word *always* is an example of exaggeration. The belief that a person must or is able to be perfect every single minute is not based on facts and cannot be proven. Mistakes are a natural part of life.

Am I awfulizing?

Informed choice makers know that using the word *awful* is an example of stretching the truth. They might prefer to be perfect, but they cannot prove that it is awful if they are not 100% perfect all the time. The worst thing that might happen if they were to make a mistake would be that they might have to correct that mistake. They cannot prove that that would be so awful.

CHANGE ASSUMPTION Students develop a new belief that can be proved:

> "I do not have to be perfect."

THE PROVABLE
BELIEF

ACT ON NEW BELIEF Ask students to think of ways that they can help themselves think, feel, and behave according to the new belief.

Feeling

—Observe their bodies and ask themselves what they are feeling, for example, despair, hopelessness, inadequacy.

Thinking

—Observe their thoughts and identify their self-talk, for example, "I must be perfect, I can never make a mistake or it's awful, and I'm a failure."

Behaving

—Change their self-talk to go along with the provable belief. "I do not have to be perfect. It is O.K. to make mistakes along the way, and it does not mean that I'm a failure."

Take Action

—Look at the mistake to find out what they might do differently the next time; be proud of their successes, even when they are not perfect.

5. Revise the scene:

PREPARE ROLES TO REFLECT NEW BELIEF

Thoughts

—It is not awful if I make a mistake. I can try my best and learn from what I did wrong without feeling like a failure.

Feelings

—hope, calmness, curiosity

Behaviors

—deep breathing, thinking about the assignment, erasing mistakes

CREATE A STORY LINE AND IDEAS FOR DIALOGUE

The teacher announces that there is to be an in-class assignment that must be completed in 15 minutes. "Class, here is your assignment. I'd like you to complete it before we leave for recess."

As the assignment is given out, we hear the thoughts of a student, Marv. "I want to do well on this assignment, so I'm going to

EXAMPLE STORY LINE
"PERFECT OR NOT?"
REVISED SCENE

> take a deep breath and try my best." The student takes several deep breaths and begins the assignment. He makes a mistake and takes another deep breath as a reminder not to get upset about it. He then erases the error, completes the assignment, and turns it in. Both student and teacher are pleased that the work has been turned in.

6. Ask students to act out the revised scene with the changes caused by changing the assumption. Remind them to use their own dialogue and gestures to show how they are feeling and what they are thinking.

REFLECTIVE DETECTIVE   Have students choose an art form in which they feel the least proficient. Options include music, dance, and visual art. Ask them to create a brief project of their choice, for example, a song, dance, or drawing, and to work on staying relaxed and enjoying the process rather than creating a masterful product. Ask them to share their project as well as their feelings about the process with another student.

A week after this lesson, give students an opportunity to share highlights from their handout and to discuss experiences that they had with perfectionism during the week.

Primary Grade Modifications

SCENE INVESTIGATION—Change situation to trying to color a picture with exactly the right colors and staying only within the lines.

Middle and High School Modifications

SCENE INVESTIGATION—Increase the tension in the situation by adding the element that the student needs to be perfect every time, for example, he or she needs to get an A+ with every single answer correct, every time.

This lesson explores choices and assumptions people make in their relationships with others. Students learn to apply self-awareness and emotional self-control to building healthy relationships. As choices and assumptions are examined and social skills built, students develop a sense of empathy and a growing ability to handle relationships effectively.

PROMOTING FRIENDSHIP

There are many ways to behave with friends. Some people hardly ever question how they act with their friends, behaving mostly out of habit. The need for friendship is so strong that many people may be pulled to make ineffective choices to gain or keep friends. Because some of these behaviors are more helpful than others, informed choice makers want to choose those that are most helpful in becoming and having good friends.

Lesson 13 examines assumptions and choices made about friendship. Activity 1 explores students' beliefs about their choices regarding friendship. Activity 2 builds students' skills in distinguishing between positive and negative friendship behaviors. Activity 3 explores the assumption "I will never be able to do anything to be a better friend" through a scene.

Additional ways to promote positive friendship choices are sharing choices you have made and discussing choices you observe students making.

Promoting Friendship

LESSON 13

TARGETED EMOTIONAL DOMAINS Self-Awareness, Managing Emotions, Self-Control, Empathy, Handling Relationships

TARGETED INTELLIGENCES Verbal/Linguistic, Visual/Spatial, Logical/Mathematical, Bodily/Kinesthetic, Intrapersonal, Interpersonal, Musical/Rhythmic

CURRICULAR AREAS Health, Language Arts, Social Studies, Math, Music

▶ Activity 1: FRIENDSHIP CHOICES

1. Explain that this activity examines some behaviors toward friends.

2. Tell students that you will read descriptions of behaviors toward a friend. After you read a description, students decide whether they think that behavior would help them to be a good friend or whether that behavior would not help them to be a good friend.

3. After each description is read, students vote by raising their hands when you say *help* if they believe that behavior would help them to be a good friend, or after you say *not help* if they believe that behavior would not help them to be a good friend. Examples of descriptions that you might use for this activity include

—accepting that not all your friends need to act exactly like you do

—believing that all your friends need to act exactly like you do

—showing off

—sharing your skills

—talking to your friends only about your problems

—sharing the good and the bad

—talking about how you feel

—taking your feelings out on your friends

—never talking to somebody new

—reaching out and saying hello

—really listening to others

—paying attention only to your own thoughts

—buying a friend

—making friends by being yourself

▶ Activity 2: INQUIRY

1. Prepare the Friendship Check form by using the three column format (see Blacklines). Write the title at the top of the page. Label the columns *Day, Positive Choice,* and *Negative Choice.* Add the direction: "Fill in the day and check under 'Positive Choice' if you made a positive behavior choice that day regarding your friends or 'Negative Choice' if you made a negative choice that day regarding your friends."

2. Ask students to complete the inquiry sentence—"One way that I now act with my friends is that I . . . ." on the Friendship handout (see Blacklines).

3. Introduce the Friendship Check form and ask students to fill it out during the week.

▶ Activity 3: SCENE INVESTIGATION: BEING FRIENDS

1. Tell students that this scene investigates qualities of friendship by examining the assumption:

THE ASSUMPTION

> "I will never be able to do anything to be a better friend."

Create a suitable scene, using the example scene as a reference.

2. Develop a scene:

CHOOSE A SITUATION lecture about friendship by two experts. One expert speaks about and demonstrates the impossibility of doing anything to become a better friend and the other about the possibility of becoming a better friend.

ESTABLISH SETTING a college lecture hall

IDENTIFY CHARACTERS a host professor, two guest lecturers, student assistants, and the audience

PREPARE ROLES TO REFLECT ASSUMPTION

Thoughts

—We act with our friends the way we do because we have always done it that way. Whatever happens as a result happens, and there's nothing we can do about it.

Feelings

—resignation, frustration

CREATE A STORY LINE AND IDEAS FOR DIALOGUE

EXAMPLE STORY LINE "BEING FRIENDS"

The hosting professor introduces one of the guest lecturers to the audience. "I am very honored to present Mr. Friendship No-Choice. He will speak to us about how we cannot change our behavior with our friends and how we just have to accept our lots. Class, I give you Mr. Friendship No-Choice."

"Thank you, Professor. I have asked several of your fellow students to demonstrate the points I will be making by acting them out for you. Today we look at 'buying friends.' Someone who buys a friend offers another person something in exchange for that person's friendship. Quite often, that person only appears to be a friend, and in reality, is only interested in what is being offered. My student assistants will now demonstrate an example of buying a friend."

One student, Hasan, approaches another, Charlie, pretending to be on the playground at recess. We hear Hasan's thoughts as he approaches Charlie. "I know this kid hardly ever talks to me, but I'd like to be his friend. Maybe if I gave him my candy, he'd like me better. It usually gets people to pay attention to me."

Hasan says aloud, "Hey, I've got some candy in my pocket. You want some?" We hear the thoughts of Charlie, the student being approached. "I don't know this guy. I don't even know if I like him, but I sure like his candy." Charlie says aloud, "Sure kid, I'll take it."

Hasan gives him the candy and says, "Hey, you want to play some ball or something?" Charlie finishes the candy and says, "Look, I have to go over there and play in that game they're setting up. But call me if you get some more candy, O.K.?" He walks away as the first student watches him sadly.

Mr. Friendship No-Choice says, "The student tried to buy a friend and ended up sad and alone with an empty bag of candy. And I, Mr. Friendship No-Choice, am here to tell you that there is nothing in the world Hasan can do to change that. He always has tried to make friends that way and he always will try to make friends that way. Whatever happens, happens, and there is nothing he can do to change that. I thank you."

3. Enact the scene: Students act out the scene, using their own dialogue and behaviors and expressing their own thoughts and feelings about the position.

4. Reflect on the enactment:

THE ASSUMPTION
EXAMINED

EXAMINE ASSUMPTION Remind students that the assumption that was used here was "I will never be able to do anything to be a better friend." Have students ask two of the questions for examining assumptions (Am I awfulizing? does not apply here):

Am I crystal balling?

Informed choice makers know that it is impossible to predict what someone will or will not be able to do in the future. It might be easier to keep on acting the same way all the time, relying on habits rather than choices. However, it is not based on fact to say that one will never be able to do anything to be a better friend in the future.

Am I generalizing?

Informed choice makers know that it is exaggerating to use the word *never*. It might not be easy to do the things it might take to be a better friend. However, it is stretching the truth to say that one could never do those things.

CHANGE ASSUMPTION Students develop a new belief about friendship that would be provable:

"There are some things I can do to be a better friend."

ACT ON NEW BELIEF Have students consider ways in which they might feel or behave that would help them act according to the new belief.

Feeling

—Observe their bodies and ask themselves what they are feeling, for example, frustrated, lonely.

Thinking

—Observe their thoughts and ask themselves to identify their self-talk, for example, "I don't like not having friends, but there is nothing I can do or will ever be able to do about it."

Behaving

—Change their self-talk to go along with the provable belief. For example, "I don't like not having friends and there are some things I can do about it. It may not be easy to change old habits, but it is possible."

Take Action

—Try new friendship choices such as introducing themselves to others and joining in conversations already started by first listening and then adding their ideas to what is being discussed.

5. Revise the scene:

PREPARE ROLES TO REFLECT NEW BELIEF

Thoughts

—I don't like not having friends and there are some things I can do about it. I can make new choices.

Feelings

—hope

Behaviors

—introducing themselves

CREATE A STORY LINE AND IDEAS FOR DIALOGUE

The hosting professor introduces the new guest lecturer to the audience. "I am very honored to be able to present Ms. Friendship Choice. She will speak about how we can change how we behave regarding our friends. She will share her understanding that we do not have to act out of habit. We can find new ways to behave so that we can have and be better friends. Class, I give you Ms. Friendship Choice."

"Thank you, Professor. My student assistants will demonstrate behaviors relating to the same issue that Mr. Friendship No-Choice discussed. We will demonstrate and discuss buying friends."

One student, Laila, approaches another student, Margarita, pretending to be on the playground at recess. We hear Laila's thoughts as she approaches: "I know this girl hardly ever talks to me but I'd like to be her friend. I sometimes can get kids to pay attention to me by giving them things like candy. At least they'll talk to me, but only really for the candy, not because they're my friend. This girl might not talk to me if I don't offer her something, but I want her to like me for myself. It might not work, but I'm going to try just going up and talking to her and hope that she likes me for me and not for what I can give her." She approaches Margarita. "Hi. I know we haven't talked that much so far this year, so I thought I'd be the first to say hello. Do you want to play something?" Margarita answers, "I wanted to talk to you too, but I didn't know what to say. I thought you'd think I was dumb or something. Why don't we go and play on the swings?" They both walk away, smiling.

Ms. Friendship Choice says, "I am here to tell you that we don't have to act out of habit. We can find new ways to act so that we can have and be better friends. I thank you and wish you many happy friendships!"

6. Have students act out the revised scene using their own words, thoughts, and feelings.

REFLECTIVE DETECTIVE

Write and perform a friendship rap, song, or jingle including all the points discussed in the friendship lesson. Group students with others who are not close friends. Ask them to share what they learned about themselves from working with their group.

About a week after this lesson, give students the opportunity to share highlights from their handouts and to discuss the different ways they behaved regarding friends during the week.

Primary Grade Modifications

FRIENDSHIP CHOICES—Add examples such as pushing someone, getting in front of someone in line, bossing someone around, taking someone's things, keeping your hands to yourself, and asking for things.

Middle and High School Modifications

FRIENDSHIP CHOICES—Add examples such as putting someone down, dressing like everyone else, taking a drink or a drug just once, and cheating or lying for someone. Also discuss the difficulties with staying true to your own ideals when the friendship stakes are so high.

SCENE INVESTIGATION—Change the situation to one in which a "friendship expert" speaks on a talk show.

STRENGTHEN-ING FAMILY

A family is made up of a group of people, all of whom have different ways of thinking, expressing feelings, and behaving, based on their own assumptions and choices. Every member of a family plays an important part, doing the tasks that need to be done and trying to get along with one another.

Sometimes family members get along easily and well with one another, and sometimes they get along with more difficulty. There are behavior choices that can be made that can help families get along better; and there are those that can make it more difficult to get along.

Lesson 14 continues building relationship skills by examining assumptions and choices made about one's family. Activity 1 is the construction of a web to explore the nature of being a child in a family. Activity 2 consists of a guided fantasy designed to sensitize students to the needs and feelings of their parents. Activity 3 builds awareness of students' behavior as a family member. Activity 4 explores the assumption "I will never be able to do anything to be a better family member" through a scene.

Additional ways to promote positive family choices are sharing personal experiences and discussing students' choices as they come up.

LESSON 14

Strengthening Family

TARGETED EMOTIONAL DOMAINS Self-Awareness, Managing Emotions, Self-Control, Empathy, Handling Relationships

TARGETED INTELLIGENCES Verbal/Linguistic, Visual/Spatial, Logical/Mathematical, Bodily/Kinesthetic, Intrapersonal, Interpersonal

CURRICULAR AREAS Health, Social Studies, Language Arts, Math

▶ Activity 1: ATTRIBUTE WEB

1. Explain to students that they are to create a web that shows the attributes of a chosen character or role that they have in the world.

2. Hand out paper and pencils.

3. Ask students to draw a circle and put the word *child* in the center.

4. Tell them that they are to draw lines coming from the outside of the circle, like a spider web. On the lines, they are to write as many things as they can

think of that describe what it is like to be a child in a family. Include things they like about it as well as things they do not like. Examples of attributes include

Like

—having meals made for me

—having someone who makes sure that I have everything I need

—being able to play

Dislike

—being told when I have to go to bed

—having to eat things I don't like

—not being taken seriously

▶ Activity 2: GUIDED FANTASY

1. Explain that this activity asks students to imagine they are someone else.

2. Ask students to close their eyes and listen to you. As they listen, they are to picture in their minds what you are describing.

3. Ask them to imagine, that they are either their father or their mother. They should imagine the things their parent does and the way he or she feels from moment to moment. Have them imagine the first thing their parent does after waking up. Is it make the beds? Get ready for work? Get the children ready for school? Prepare breakfast for the family? Tell them to picture their parent doing his or her activities. Tell students to imagine what goes through a parent's mind and pay attention to what he or she is thinking about and might be feeling. Is their parent worried about having so much to do? Calm?

4. Now ask students to picture the parent doing his or her next activity. Is it cleaning and doing laundry? Is the parent at work? What does the parent have to get done before the end of the day? Students should pay attention to what he or she is thinking and feeling. Is the washing machine broken and is the parent frustrated? Is the parent's boss angry at him or her for something the parent did not finish on time? What is he or she thinking and feeling?

5. Now have students imagine what the parent is doing at the end of the day. What still has to be done before going to bed? What is the parent thinking and feeling?

6. Have students return to themselves and open their eyes.

METACOGNITIVE
DISCUSSION What did the students learn about the things their parents do, think, and feel? What do they think they would like and dislike about being a parent in a family? For example, would they like making a difference in their children's lives? Would they dislike all the responsibilities?

▶ Activity 3: INQUIRY

1. Prepare the Family Check form by using the three column format (see Blacklines). Write the title at the top of the page. Label columns *Day, Positive Choice,* and *Negative Choice.* Add the direction: "Fill in the day then mark under 'Positive Choice' if you made a positive behavior choice that day regarding your family or under 'Negative Choice' if you made a negative behavior choice regarding your family."

2. Ask students to complete the inquiry sentence—"One way that I now act with my family is that I . . . ." on the Family handout (see Blacklines).

3. Introduce the Family Check form and ask students to fill it out during the week.

▶ Activity 4: SCENE INVESTIGATION: BEING FAMILY

1. Tell students that they are going to develop a scene about being family. The assumption that they are examining in the scene is

THE ASSUMPTION

> "I will never be able to do anything to be a better family member."

Create a suitable scene using the lesson scene as an example.

2. Develop a scene:

CHOOSE A SITUATION two episodes of two television shows depicting two different families—The More Difficult family and the Get Along Better family

ESTABLISH SETTING the kitchen table in the family home

IDENTIFY CHARACTERS child, mother, and father

PREPARE ROLES TO REFLECT ASSUMPTION

Thoughts

—Whatever happens in our family happens because we have always done things that way. There is nothing we can do to change that. We just have to accept the things we do not like and the problems we have.

Feelings

—resignation, frustration

Behaviors

—ignoring, accusing, arguing

CREATE A STORY LINE AND IDEAS FOR DIALOGUE

The More Difficult family is seated at the kitchen table, finishing dinner. Mother thinks, "I want my child to get to bed early tonight, and I know when I tell her, the same thing will happen that always does. I've just got to get her to bed. " Mother says, "You're going to bed early tonight, and I don't want to hear another word about it."

The daughter continues to eat her meal, pretending not to have heard her mother.

Father thinks, "Oh terrific, here we go again. I come home from a long day at work and have to face the same family problems every night." He says, "Can't you control your daughter? Listen, your mother told you to go to bed and that's the way it's going to be, young lady."

The daughter thinks, "They always tell me what to do, and there's never any good reason why I should. They don't care about what I want to do." She says, "You only care about what you want. You don't care about me."

Mother thinks, "Here we go again, it always ends up this way." She says, "That's it, young lady. Up to your room."

EXAMPLE STORY LINE "BEING FAMILY"

3. Enact the scene: Students act out the scene using their own dialogue and behaviors.

4. Reflect on the enactment:

EXAMINE ASSUMPTION Remind students that the assumption being enacted was "I will never be able to do anything to be a better family member." Have students ask two of the assumption examining questions (Am I awfulizing? does not apply):

THE ASSUMPTION EXAMINED

Am I crystal balling?

Informed choice makers know that it is impossible to predict what someone will or will not be able to do in the future. It might be easier to keep on acting the same way all the time, relying on habit rather than choice. However, it is not based on fact to say that one will never be able to do anything to be a better family member in the future.

Am I generalizing?

Informed choice makers know that it is exaggerating to use the word *never*. It might not be easy to do the things it might take to be a better family member. However, it is stretching the truth to say that one could never do those things.

CHANGE ASSUMPTION Students suggest a revised belief relating to the family:

THE PROVABLE
BELIEF

> ## "There are some things I can do to be a better family member."

ACT ON NEW BELIEF Students suggest feelings and behaviors that might help them to act according to the new belief:

Feeling

—Observe their bodies and ask themselves what they are feeling, such as resignation or frustration.

Thinking

—Observe their thoughts and ask themselves to identify their self-talk. For example, "I don't always like the things that go on in my family, but there is nothing I can do or will ever be able to do about it."

Behaving

—Change their self-talk to go along with the provable belief. For example: "There are some things I can do to be a better family member and change some of the things that go on in my family. It may not be easy, but it is possible."

Take Action

—Try new family choices.

5. Revise the scene:

PREPARE ROLES TO REFLECT NEW BELIEF

Feelings

—hope

Thoughts

—Maybe I don't have to react with anger. Maybe if I talked about how I felt, I could work things out.

Behaviors

—thinking before talking, expressing feelings, negotiating

CREATE A STORY LINE AND IDEAS FOR DIALOGUE

The Get Along Better family is seated at the kitchen table finishing dinner. Mother thinks, "I want my child to go to bed early tonight, and I don't want the same thing to happen that always happens when I tell her. I wonder if it might help if I explained why I wanted her to go to bed early."

Mother says, "I know you enjoy staying up and watching television. But during the past few days, you seem to have had a harder and harder time concentrating on your homework. I'm also worried about that gymnastics show you have coming up and I don't want you to hurt yourself because you're tired. I think it would be a good idea if you got to bed a little earlier tonight."

The daughter looks up at mother and thinks, "Mom never before told me the reasons why she wants me to do certain things. I still would prefer to stay up, but she kind of makes sense too."

While the daughter is thinking, father thinks, "She hasn't said anything in response to her mother, but I don't think she's ignoring her. It looks like she listened." He says, "We both want to make sure everything goes well for you. I know it's difficult to go to bed when there are things you'd rather do but we think it's important, for now."

Daughter thinks, "I could make a big fuss about this, but that only makes everyone angry. Maybe I could tell them how I feel and see if we could work this out." She says, "It is hard to go to bed as early as you want me to because that means I only have time to do my homework, eat supper, and go to sleep. Couldn't I stay up for a half an hour and then go to sleep?"

Mother says, "That sounds fair to me. I'm so glad we found a way to understand each other and work this out."

EXAMPLE STORY LINE
"BEING FAMILY"
REVISED SCENE

6. Have students enact the new scene with their own dialogue and actions.

Students create two cartoons of their family. One cartoon shows communication between family members at its worst, and the other, communication at its best.

About a week after this lesson, give students the opportunity to share highlights from their handouts and to discuss behavior choices they made regarding their families during the week.

REFLECTIVE
DETECTIVE

SkyLight Training and Publishing Inc.

Primary Grade Modifications

ATTRIBUTE WEB—Do this on the board using suggestions from students. Give examples first.

GUIDED FANTASY—Give examples first of what parents might think and feel.

SCENE INVESTIGATION—Change the revised scene in the example so that mom's concerns focus on the child's crankiness, health, and gymnastics show. Have the child talk about needing time to eat supper, do her chores, and play.

REFLECTIVE DETECTIVE—Have students draw a family portrait, show it to the class, and share something nice that each family member would say to another.

Middle and High School Modifications

ATTRIBUTE WEB—Make a second web for parents.

GUIDED FANTASY—Follow up with a revised version of the parent web based on students' new discoveries.

SCENE INVESTIGATION—Change the first scene so that the bedtime argument focuses on getting the daughter to go to bed before midnight. Change the revised scene so that the mother is concerned over slipping grades, frequent illness, and the upcoming SAT exam. Have the daughter talk about needing time for homework, job, social life, and relaxation.

Developing Emotional Intelligence Through

EMPATHY

Chapter 4 expands on the concepts in Chapter 3 by exploring choices made regarding acceptance of others.

Three lessons examine skills and behaviors needed to develop interpersonal intelligence and build empathic understanding. Students have the opportunity to develop an awareness of how they and others react to behaviors that demonstrate both negative (put-downs) and positive (complimentary) appraisals of others. Students examine the reality of peer pressure from both the giver's and the receiver's viewpoints. The concept of prejudgment, or prejudice, is carefully thought about in the final lesson, giving students an opportunity to recognize uninformed behavior and its effects on others.

LEARNING ABOUT PUT-DOWNS

Some people assume that in order to feel good about themselves, they must make someone else feel bad about themselves. Some people sometimes put down other people in an attempt to feel better about themselves, to stop others from putting them down, to get attention, to look important, to try to gain power, or just for fun. They do not always realize the negative effect that this may have on those they put down as some of these people may choose to feel hurt, become upset, and begin to put themselves down. Also, some people have a difficult time giving or accepting compliments, a critical skill for interacting effectively with others.

Lesson 15 examines assumptions and choices made regarding put-downs. Activity 1 reinforces the skill of anxiety management through an exercise for relaxing. Activity 2 provides an opportunity for sharing put-downs and compliments that are received and for exploring the emotional consequences of each. Activity 3 builds students' skills in recognizing and handling negative and positive interactions with others. Activity 4 explores the assumption "In order to feel good about myself, I must try to make someone else feel bad about him- or herself" in a scene.

Additional ways to discourage put-downs are modeling positive behavior, listening for and discouraging put-downs in class, and offering opportunities for complimenting

---

LESSON 15

Learning About Put-Downs

TARGETED EMOTIONAL DOMAINS   Self-Awareness, Managing Emotions, Self-Control, Empathy, Handling Relationships

TARGETED INTELLIGENCES   Verbal/Linguistic, Visual/Spatial, Logical/Mathematical, Bodily/Kinesthetic, Intrapersonal, Interpersonal, Musical/Rhythmic

CURRICULAR AREAS   Health, Social Studies, Language Arts, Math, Music

---

▶ Activity 1: TENSE/RELAX

Do the exercise described in Lesson 12, Activity 1. Metacognitive discussion might ask students how much they were able to relax using the exercise this time. Have they used this or other relaxation exercises on their own? What could they be doing to help themselves stay relaxed even more?

▶ Activity 2: PUT-DOWN/COMPLIMENT CIRCLE

1. Explain that a *put-down* is a negative statement about someone, which is meant to make that person feel bad, and that a *compliment* is a positive statement made about someone, which is meant to help that person feel good.

2. Tell students that they are going to do an activity that shows the effect that put-downs and compliments can have on people.

3. Form students into a circle. Explain that each member of the circle is to state one put-down that he or she has either given or received at some point in his or her life. As each person states the put-down, the rest of the circle members are to show with their bodies what they might feel like if that put-down were directed toward them.

4. After going around the circle once for the put-downs, tell students that now each one in the circle is to state one compliment he or she has either given or received at some point in his or her life. As each person states the compliment, the rest show with their bodies what it might feel like if that compliment were directed toward them.

Ask students what they felt like when they stated a put-down. What did they feel when they heard the put-down? What did they feel when they stated a compliment? What did they feel when they heard the compliment?

METACOGNITIVE
DISCUSSION

▶ Activity 3: INQUIRY

1. Prepare the Put-Down Check form by using the three column format (see Blacklines). Write the title at the top of the page. Label the columns *Day, Put-Down,* and *Helped.* Add the direction: "Fill in the day and mark under 'Put-Down' if you put someone down that day or mark under 'Helped' if you helped someone to feel good that day."

2. Ask students to complete the inquiry sentence—"A put-down I once said to someone was . . . ." on the Put-Downs handout (see Blacklines).

3. Introduce the Put-Down Check form and ask students to fill it out during the week.

▶ Activity 4: SCENE INVESTIGATION: RELATING TO OTHERS

1. Explain that the students are creating a scene to investigate the effects of

---

different ways to relate to others, particularly using put-downs and giving compliments. The assumption that is being examined is

THE ASSUMPTION

> "In order to feel good about myself, I must try to make someone else feel bad about him- or herself."

Create a suitable scene, using the example scene as a model.

2. Develop a scene:

CHOOSE A SITUATION one youngster watches and comments as another youngster struggles in math class

ESTABLISH SETTING a classroom

IDENTIFY CHARACTERS a struggling student, a commenting student, teacher, and fellow classmates

PREPARE ROLES TO REFLECT ASSUMPTION

Thoughts

—I can't believe he doesn't know the answers. Everybody will laugh and know how smart I am if I show them how dumb he is.

Feelings

—disdain, fear

Behaviors

—putting the struggling student down, pointing out his difficulties to the rest of the class, showing off by telling how he knows all of the right answers

CREATE A STORY LINE AND IDEAS FOR DIALOGUE

EXAMPLE STORY LINE
"RELATING TO OTHERS"

The teacher has called on a student to answer a particular math problem. "Would you please give us the answer?"

The student, Juan, thinks, "I wish I hadn't been called on. I really don't know the answer. I hope nobody makes fun of me. Maybe if I stall long enough, the teacher will move on."

Another student, Niels, watches and notices that his classmate is struggling. He thinks, "He doesn't know the answer. Everyone in class will laugh and think I'm so smart if I show them how dumb he is." Niels says, "You don't know the answer, do you? Boy, are you dumb. I bet when they gave out brains, you thought they said trains and passed them up."

> The teacher looks at Niels with frustration, and says, "I'll deal with you during recess."
>
> Juan thinks, "Maybe he's right. I don't always know the answers. Maybe I am dumb." He tries to talk positively to himself, but has a hard time believing himself. He stays quiet for the rest of class, unsure of himself.

3. Enact the scene: Have students act out the scene using their own thoughts, dialogue, and behaviors.

4. Reflect on the enactment:

   EXAMINE ASSUMPTION Remind students that the assumption being investigated was "In order to feel good about myself, I must try to make someone else feel bad about him- or herself." Have them ask two questions about assumptions (Am I awfulizing? does not apply):

   THE ASSUMPTION EXAMINED

Am I crystal balling?

Informed choice makers know that is impossible to predict how one will feel about oneself in the future. Even if one were to succeed in making someone feel bad about him- or herself, it is not possible to predict that this would definitely lead to one feeling good about oneself. It might even lead to one feeling bad about oneself.

Am I generalizing?

Informed choice makers know that it is exaggerating to use the word *must*. It is not based on fact to think that the only way to feel good about oneself is to try to make someone else feel bad about him- or herself. People have control over their choices about what they can do in order to feel good about themselves, including empathizing with others' feelings and giving themselves or others a compliment. It is possible for them to feel good about themselves at the same time that others are feeling good about themselves.

CHANGE ASSUMPTION A possible new belief is

THE PROVABLE BELIEF

> "I don't have to try to make others feel bad about themselves in order to feel good about myself."

ACT ON NEW BELIEF Students might do several things:

Feeling

—Observe their bodies and ask themselves what they are feeling, such as disdain or fear.

Thinking

—Observe their thoughts and ask themselves to identify their self-talk, for example, "The class will see how funny and smart I am if I make them see how dumb he is."

Behaving

—Change their self-talk to go along with the provable belief, for example, "I don't feel any better about myself when I try to make someone else feel bad about him- or herself. The person may feel bad, but that doesn't help me to feel good about myself. Maybe there are other things I can try to feel good about myself."

Take Action

—Empathize with others' feelings, give themselves a compliment, try to help another person to do better and feel good about him- or herself.

5. Revise the scene:

PREPARE ROLES TO REFLECT NEW BELIEF

Thoughts

—I can find all kinds of ways to feel good about myself, including helping another to feel good about him- or herself.

Feelings

—confidence, satisfaction

Behaviors

—giving encouragement, asking the teacher if he can help the struggling student

CREATE A STORY LINE AND IDEAS FOR DIALOGUE

EXAMPLE STORY LINE
"RELATING TO OTHERS"
REVISED SCENE

The teacher has called on a student to answer a particular math problem. "Would you please give us the answer?"

The student, Juan, thinks, "I wish I hadn't been called on. I really don't know the answer."

Another student, Niels, is watching and notices his classmate is struggling. Niels thinks, "It would be a real easy laugh and a way to show off if I made fun of him. But that will only make him feel bad and nobody will really know that I have the answer. Maybe I could try to help him out. He'd feel better and everyone would see that I'm smart, and that would feel good." Niels looks over at Juan, smiles, and says, "Come on, you can do it. You know the answer." The classmate smiles back, thinks hard, and still can't come up with the answer.

Niels asks the teacher, "May I help him with the answer?" The teacher says, "That would be very nice of you." Niels leans over and whispers a hint into his classmate's ear.

Juan smiles and says, "The answer is twenty-four!" All look smart and feel good about themselves, and the class is happy.

6. Have students act out the scene using their own dialogue and actions.

Divide into groups and create and then perform a song in honor of the other group. Be sure to include one positive statement about each member of the group.

About a week following this lesson, give students the opportunity to share highlights from their handouts and to discuss their experiences with put-downs during the week.

REFLECTIVE
DETECTIVE

Primary Grade Modifications

SCENE INVESTIGATION—Change the task the student is struggling with to a basic skill such as identifying letters, numbers, or shapes.

METACOGNITIVE DISCUSSION—Lead students in creating a song.

Middle and High School Modifications

PUT-DOWN/COMPLIMENT CIRCLE—Do this activity on paper if your students would find it difficult sharing these thoughts aloud.

SCENE INVESTIGATION—Change the situation to that of a student, Sue, watching and commenting as a new student, Dina, comes into the room.

DEALING WITH PEER PRESSURE

This lesson considers two ways that peer pressure can affect a person. In one way, someone may use peer pressure to coerce someone else. Sometimes, some people make the choice to try to get others to do what they would like them to do by putting pressure on them in a number of different ways, such as being bossy, teasing, bribing, or threatening. Sometimes they do this as part of a group, and sometimes they do it by themselves. They do not always realize the negative effects of their pressuring another person and how bad the person being pressured may feel.

The second way peer pressure may be viewed is from the perspective of the person being pressured. Some people might feel pressured to do things that others tell them to do, allowing others to determine choices they make. Sometimes they base their definition of "cool" on others' assumptions or on assumptions they have developed. There are a number of qualities they assume they must have and a number of actions they assume they must take in order to be cool. They might feel pressured to do these things in order to be thought cool. They do not always examine these assumptions to determine whether the assumptions are based on facts. Sometimes what seems to be cool at first glance turns out to be not cool when examined more thoroughly.

Some people might give in to pressures to act in a certain way because they are afraid that others might not like them if they do not do so. They might believe that it is important to be liked by everyone. They may believe that if they do not give into pressuring, they will not be liked and that would be awful.

Lesson 16 examines choices and assumptions related to peer pressure. Activity 1 provides a kinesthetic understanding of the nature of pressuring. Activity 2 explores examples of pressuring through communication. Activity 3 builds students' skills in recognizing and quashing their own activities that pressure others. Activity 4 explores the assumption "I must pressure others in order to always have my way, or it will be awful" through a scene. Activity 5 explores students' definitions of cool. Activity 6 builds students' awareness and ability to resist pressuring from others. Activity 7 explores the assumption "I must give in to pressure to be cool and be liked by everyone, or it will be awful" in a scene. Note that activities for each side of the competence are arranged together (Activities 1 through 4 for pressuring a peer and Activities 5 through 7 for being pressured). At your discretion, you may choose to present the two Inquiry activities at the same time and mix the other activities as you think best, although I recommend doing the two Scene Investigations separately.

Additional ways to discourage pressuring others are personal modeling and watching for and discouraging examples of pressuring. Discourage acceptance of pressure by modeling, sharing personal stories, and watching for and discouraging acceptance of pressure while encouraging assertiveness and independent choices.

Dealing With Peer Pressure

LESSON
16

TARGETED EMOTIONAL DOMAINS Self-Awareness, Managing Emotions, Self-Control, Empathy, Handling Relationships

TARGETED INTELLIGENCES Verbal/Linguistic, Visual/Spatial, Logical/Mathematical, Bodily/Kinesthetic, Intrapersonal, Interpersonal, Naturalist

CURRICULAR AREAS Health, Language Arts, Social Studies, Math, Science

▶ Activity 1: FORTRESS

1. Tell students, except for one, that they are to all join hands in a circle.

2. Ask the single student to try to join the circle while everyone in the circle tries to keep the student out. The joining student is not to use physical force to get into the circle. (Have several students try to enter the circle.)

3. How did each student try to get into the circle? Was pressure involved? In what ways?

▶ Activity 2: PRESSURING CIRCLE

1. Explain that *pressuring* is when we try to get someone to do something we would like them to do in a way that leads them to feel that they have no choice but to go along with what we want.

2. With students still in the circle from Activity 1, ask each student in the circle to give an example of something that someone might be pressured to do and how that pressuring might be communicated. For example,

   —pressuring someone to play a game I want to play by saying that he won't be my friend any more if he doesn't play

   —pressuring someone to give me her lunch money by threatening to punch her

   —pressuring someone to give me his or her homework by promising to be his or her best friend.

▶ Activity 3: INQUIRY

1. Prepare the Pressuring Check form by using the three column format (see Blacklines). Write the title at the top of the page. Label the columns *Day,*

Pressured, and *Asked.* Add the direction: "Fill in the day and mark under 'Pressured' if you pressured some one to get what you wanted that day or mark under 'Asked' if you asked directly for what you wanted that day."

2. Ask students to complete the inquiry sentence—"A time I pressured someone was when . . . ." on the Pressuring handout (see Blacklines).

3. Introduce the Pressuring Check form and ask students to fill it out during the week.

▶ Activity 4: SCENE INVESTIGATION: PRESSURING PEERS

1. Explain that the students are to create a scene that illustrates the following assumption:

THE ASSUMPTION

> "I must pressure others in order to always have my way, or it will be awful."

Create a suitable scene, using the example scene as a reference.

2. Develop a scene:

CHOOSE A SITUATION a king commands his subjects to give him their Twinkies from their lunches or the king will banish them from the kingdom of Cool

ESTABLISH SETTING the castle lunchroom

IDENTIFY CHARACTERS the king and some royal subjects with Twinkies

PREPARE ROLES TO REFLECT ASSUMPTION

Thoughts

—I must use everything in my power to show everyone who's in charge. I must have my way no matter what anyone else wants or feels.

Feelings

—worried, insecure

Behaviors

—bribing, demanding, threatening

CREATE A STORY LINE AND IDEAS FOR DIALOGUE

EXAMPLE STORY LINE "PRESSURING PEERS"

The King of Cool is surrounded by his subjects. He makes a proclamation. "All royal subjects who wish to get on the good side of the king will relinquish their Twinkies to him." His hungry royal subjects continue to eat, knowing that once their Twinkies are devoured, the king will forget all about them.

King Cool thinks, "I must have my way. What can I do to force them to give me what I want? Maybe if I focus on one of my weaker subjects, he'll give in." He calls Ronald, one of his subjects, to him. "I bid you come to me this instant." Ronald comes to him, thinking, "What does the king want from me? I want the king to like me."

King Cool thinks, "This will get him," and says to Ronald, "You will turn over your Twinkie to me immediately or I will banish you from the kingdom of Cool. Unless you do as I say, I won't like you and you will never be cool or popular again."

Ronald thinks to himself, "I'm really hungry, but I can't be banished from Cool. That would be terrible. I'd hate it if the king didn't like me." "All right, your majesty, have my Twinkie."

The other royal subjects, seeing what the king is doing, speak among themselves. "Our king is so sneaky. I wish he would just ask for what he wants without being so bossy. None of us like him. I wonder if he even cares." Feeling bad for Ronald, who gave up his Twinkie, they call him over and share their Twinkies with him gladly. They all watch the king as he finishes his Twinkie and sits all alone, with a glimmer of sadness in his eyes.

3. Enact the scene: Have students act out the scene using their own dialogue and behaviors to show what the characters might do, think, and feel.

4. Reflect on the enactment:

EXAMINE ASSUMPTION Remind students that the assumption being portrayed was "I must pressure others in order to always have my way, or it will be awful." They ask themselves the three assumption examining questions:

THE ASSUMPTION
EXAMINED

Am I crystal balling?

Informed choice makers know that it is impossible to predict how it would be if they did not use pressure and did not always get their way. There are many possibilities as to how it might be. It might be not to their liking, or it might even be just fine. However, they cannot prove that it would be awful.

Am I generalizing?

Informed choice makers know that using the words *must* and *always* are examples of generalizing. They might want to use pressure in order to have their way as often as possible. However, there are other options to try to get things that are wanted, such as asking directly. It is stretching the truth to say that they must pressure others to have their way always.

Am I awfulizing?

Informed choice makers know that it is an exaggeration to believe that something awful would happen if they did not pressure or did not have their way. The worst that might happen would be that they might not get exactly what they wanted at that particular moment. They might prefer that this were not so, but it is not based on facts to say that this would be awful.

CHANGE ASSUMPTION The new belief becomes

THE PROVABLE BELIEF

> "I do not have to pressure others to have my way."

ACT ON NEW BELIEF Students might do several things:

Feeling

—Observe their bodies and ask themselves what they are feeling, for example, worried or insecure.

Thinking

—Observe their thoughts and ask themselves to identify their self-talk, such as, It would be awful if I didn't have my way. The only way I can get that is by using pressure.

Behaving

—Change their self-talk to go along with the provable belief, for example, "I do not have to pressure others in order to have my way. If I did not have my way, that would not be so awful."

Take Action

—They can ask directly for what they want.

5. Revise the scene:

PREPARE ROLES TO REFLECT NEW BELIEF

Thoughts

—I don't have to use everything in my power to show everyone that I'm in charge and that I am King Cool. They already know that. I don't have to pressure others to get what I want. I can ask directly. If I'm nice about it, I might get what I want and have my subjects like me too.

Feelings

—hope, security

Behaviors

—asking directly

CREATE A STORY LINE AND IDEAS FOR DIALOGUE

> The King of Cool is surrounded by his royal subjects who are eating their lunches. The king thinks, "I'm hungry, and my chef forget to pack a Twinkie for me. I could command that my subjects give me one of theirs. But nobody likes a king who throws his weight around. I think I'll ask directly."
>
> The king says, "Royal subjects, I, the king, am hungry. My chef forgot to give me a Twinkie. I would be very grateful if one of you would share your Twinkie with me." He looks around, wondering how his subjects feel about the direct approach.
>
> Within moments, a large group of his subjects goes up to the throne, gladly offering to share their Twinkies. And all is well in the Kingdom of Cool.

EXAMPLE STORY LINE
"PRESSURING PEERS"
REVISED SCENE

6. Have students act out the new scene, using appropriate dialogue and behavior to express the belief.

Design and share a scientific experiment demonstrating pressure.

METACOGNITIVE
DISCUSSION

▶ Activity 5: COOL FORMULA

1. Explain that each student is going to write a formula for what it takes to be cool. The formula should include personal qualities and behaviors that they believe contribute to someone being thought of as cool, as well as behaviors and qualities that detract from someone's coolness.

2. When the students have finished writing, ask them to share their formula with another student or with the class.

Did everyone define cool in the same way? Who decides what is cool and what is not cool? On what is that decision based? Can one become cool? How?

METACOGNITIVE
DISCUSSION

▶ Activity 6: INQUIRY

1. Prepare the Being Pressured Check form by using the three column format (see Blacklines). Write the title at the top of the page. Label columns *Day, Gave In,* and *Own Choice.* Add directions: "Fill in the day and mark under

'Gave In' if you felt you made a choice by giving in to pressure that day or mark 'Own Choice' if you acted on your own choice that day."

2. Ask students to complete the Inquiry sentence—"A time I gave in to pressure was . . . ." on the Being Pressured handout (see Blacklines).

3. Introduce the Being Pressured Check form and ask students to fill it out during the week.

▶ Activity 7: SCENE INVESTIGATION: BEING PRESSURED BY PEERS

1. Explain that the assumption they will explore in this activity is

THE ASSUMPTION

> "I must give in to pressure to be cool and to be liked by everyone, or it will be awful."

It is the reverse side of the assumption in Activity 4, which took the viewpoint of a creator of pressure.

2. Develop a scene:

CHOOSE A SITUATION a girl is being pressured by her friend into trying a can of beer at a slumber party

ESTABLISH SETTING a bedroom and a kitchen

IDENTIFY CHARACTERS a girl giving the party, a girl being pressured, and other guests

PREPARE ROLES TO REFLECT ASSUMPTION

Thoughts

—I really don't want to try this beer. But if I don't drink it, she won't think I'm cool and she probably won't like me anymore. That would be awful.

Feelings

—confusion, worry

Behaviors

—trying weakly to avoid having to drink the beer, drinking the beer, becoming upset and sick

CREATE A STORY LINE AND IDEAS FOR DIALOGUE

EXAMPLE STORY LINE "BEING PRESSURED BY PEERS"

A group of girls is sitting on the floor of their friend's bedroom, talking and eating potato chips. One of the girls says to the girl who is hosting the slumber party, "Is there anything to drink? These chips have made me thirsty." The hostess says, "I don't know, but I'll go check."

The hostess goes into the kitchen to search the refrigerator for something to drink. She finds half a carton of milk, a little orange juice, and a few cans of Coke. She decides to bring in the cans of Coke. As she is reaching for the last can, she notices a can of beer toward the back of the refrigerator. She thinks, "I wonder what this tastes like. Mom wouldn't notice if one little can was gone. I'll tell my friend Amy to come in here. She would try it with me." She calls out, "Amy, could you come here for a minute?"

Amy walks into the kitchen to join her friend. The hostess holds up the can of beer and says, "Hey Amy, look what I found. I think we should try some. My mother's upstairs so she'll never know."

Amy thinks, "I really don't want to try it, but she'd probably think I wasn't cool if I didn't. Maybe I can get out of having to drink it and still have her think I'm cool." Amy says, "I'm not really thirsty. Besides, there isn't a lot there. Why don't you have it all."

The hostess says, "It won't be as much fun if we don't taste it together. You're my best friend and we do everything together. You're not afraid to try it, are you?"

Amy thinks, "I don't want the beer, but if I lost a friend, that would be awful." She says, "All right, I'll try a little." The hostess gives her the can of beer, and she takes a sip. The hostess says, "Come on, you can drink more than that. It won't bite." By this time, other girls have made their way to the kitchen. One girl says, "Oh, she's not cool enough to drink the whole thing." With that, Amy drinks the whole can of beer.

The girls gather around her, asking her questions about what it tasted like and how she felt. Amy starts feeling worse and worse, upset that she did something she thought was wrong and beginning to feel sick to her stomach. In the middle of being asked one of the questions, Amy runs to the bathroom where she spends the rest of the night. Her "friend" the hostess is nowhere to be found.

3. Enact the scene: Have students act out the scene using their own words and gestures.

4. Reflect on the enactment:

EXAMINE ASSUMPTION Remind students that the assumption in this scene was "I must give in to pressure to be cool and to be liked by everyone, or it will be awful." Ask the three key questions about assumptions:

THE ASSUMPTION EXAMINED

Am I crystal balling?

Informed choice makers know that it is impossible to predict how it would be if they did not give in to pressure. They do not know for a fact that it would be awful. Nor can they prove that giving in to pressure would cause them to be cool or result in having others like them.

Am I generalizing?

Informed choice makers know that using the word *must* is an example of generalizing. They might find it easier to give in to pressure, but they cannot prove that this is their only choice as to how to be cool and have friends, and that they must do so. It is possible to find friends who would like them and find them cool when they do not give in to pressure.

Am I awfulizing?

Informed choice makers know that it is an exaggeration to believe that something awful would happen if they did not give in to pressure. The worst thing that might happen if they did not give in to someone's pressure might be that that particular person might not be their friend. They may prefer that the person were their friend, but they cannot prove that it would be awful if the person did not become a friend.

CHANGE ASSUMPTION The new belief becomes

THE PROVABLE
BELIEF

> "I do not have to give in to pressure to be cool
> and to be liked by everyone."

ACT ON NEW BELIEF Students come up with the kinds of thoughts, feelings, and behaviors that the new assumption might provide:

Feeling

—Observe their bodies and ask themselves what they are feeling, for example, confusion and worry.

Thinking

—Observe their thoughts and ask themselves to identify their self-talk, for example, "It would be awful if I wasn't thought of as cool or if I wasn't liked. The only way I can make sure those things don't happen is by giving in to pressure."

Behaving

—Change their self-talk to go along with the provable belief, such as "I do not have to give in to pressure to be cool and to have others like me. I can be cool in many other ways. Even if some people don't like me because I won't do what they want, I can find a friend who will like me even if I don't do what they want."

Take Action

—They can resist pressure by firmly saying no to what someone wants them to do and take action that shows that they mean no. They can find a friend who will like them without pressuring them.

5. Revise the scene:

PREPARE ROLES TO REFLECT NEW BELIEF

Thoughts

—I can be cool without giving in to pressure. If this friend will only like me if I give in to her pressuring, then maybe she's not a real friend. I can find a friend who will not pressure me.

Feelings

—confidence, strength

Behaviors

—firmly saying no to the drink and leaving the kitchen, finding a friend at the party who will support and not pressure

CREATE A STORY LINE AND IDEAS FOR DIALOGUE

EXAMPLE STORY LINE "BEING PRESSURED BY PEERS" REVISED SCENE

A group of girls is on the floor of their friend's bedroom, talking and eating potato chips. One of the girls says to the girl is who hosting the slumber party, "Is there anything to drink? These chips have made me thirsty." The hostess says, "I don't know, but I'll go check."

The hostess goes into the kitchen to search the refrigerator for something to drink. She finds half a carton of milk, a little orange juice, and a few cans of Coke. She decides to bring in the cans of Coke. As she reaches for the last can, she notices a can of beer toward the back of the refrigerator. She thinks, "I wonder what this tastes like. Mom wouldn't notice if one little can was gone. I'll tell my friend Amy to come in here. She'd try it with me." She calls out, "Amy, could you come here for a minute?"

Amy walks into the kitchen to join her friend. The hostess holds up the can of beer and says, "Amy, look what I found. I think we should try some. My mother's upstairs so she'll never know."

Amy thinks, "It would be easier to go along with what she wants, but I really don't want to drink this beer. She may not like it, but I'm going to tell her how I feel." Amy says, "Thanks, but I really don't want any."

The hostess says, "It won't be as much fun if we don't taste it together. You're my best friend and we do everything together. You're not afraid to try it, are you?"

Amy thinks, "I really don't want to lose her as a friend. But if that happens because I won't give in to her pressure, then maybe she's not the true friend I thought she was." She says, "You're my best friend too, but there are some things we aren't going to do together. I don't want the beer."

By this time, other girls have made their way into the kitchen. One girl says, "Oh, she's not cool enough to drink it." Amy thinks, "If she doesn't think I'm cool because of this, that wouldn't be so awful. I'm cool in a lot of other ways." She says, "I know I'm cool, so I don't have to prove it to you by doing something I don't want to do." And with that, Amy leaves the kitchen with another friend of hers who supports her in her choice.

6. Have students act out the revised scene using their own dialogue and gestures to show what the characters are thinking and feeling.

REFLECTIVE DETECTIVE Design a collage using ads that try to show what should be bought and used in order to be cool, as well as pictures and statements from this lesson.

About a week after this lesson, give students the opportunity to share highlights from their handouts and to discuss their experiences with peer pressure during the week of the lesson.

Primary Grade Modifications

PRESSURING CIRCLE—Give examples first.

COOL FORMULA—Do this as a class, offering examples such as wearing the right clothes, having a certain color hair, and being good at sports.

SCENE INVESTIGATION: BEING PRESSURED BY PEERS—Develop and enact a scene about resisting pressure based on a situation described in a student's inquiry activity. A comment about the drinking scenario: Although it would probably not arise at a very young age, the earlier youngsters are exposed to positive choices regarding drug and alcohol use, the more resistance they will have. If you choose to introduce the topic at a young age, begin the scene by briefly discussing the dangers and consequences of drinking. Also, consider reading and discussing this scene rather than acting it out. In addition, follow up this scene with several small role-plays, enacting resistance to drugs offered by strangers on a playground and offers of candy by strangers in cars.

REFLECTIVE DETECTIVE—Draw pictures that would illustrate the two scenes enacted.

Middle and High School Modifications

FORTRESS—Discuss other situations where physical force might be used, such as in sports activities, sexual encounters, and instances of abuse.

PRESSURING CIRCLE—Use examples such as pressure to use drugs or drink alcohol, pressure to have sex, pressure to do favors. Demonstrate and discuss the variety of ways that some people pressure someone, such as teasing, bribing, being bossy, and threatening.

SCENE INVESTIGATION: PRESSURING PEERS—Use the story as a fairy tale. Have the students enact their own variations on the story, replacing the Twinkie with situations from their own lives, such as pressure to lend money. Have students write and share a moral to their stories.

COOL FORMULA—Follow up with a discussion of how the requirements for and importance of being cool change in different places and times. Also discuss the connection between coolness and popularity as well as the difficulty with individuality amidst the pressure to conform.

SCENE INVESTIGATION: BEING PRESSURED BY PEERS—Change the situation to one in which a boy tries to pressure a girl into a sexual encounter.

EXAMINING PREJUDICE

Sometimes, some people may look at certain qualities or characteristics of a person or group of people and choose to make assumptions about them based only on those qualities or characteristics, overlooking other qualities and characteristics. This is particularly true when that person or group of people are different than them in some way.

Sometimes, some people choose to gossip about people who are different than themselves, spreading rumors without checking the facts. They may be afraid of those who are different or they may even believe that people who are different than them are not as good as they are.

And sometimes, there are people who feel that everyone should be exactly as they are because it is the only good and right way to be. They do not see that people are all different from each other in certain ways and that these differences can be enjoyed.

Lesson 17 examines assumptions and choices relating to prejudice. Activity 1 presents a story exploring the assumption "If someone is different from me, he or she is not as good a person as I am." Activity 2 gives students the opportunity to explore their reactions to new people and to build their ability to accept a new person who is different. Activity 3 provides an opportunity to explore the story presented in Activity 1 through role-playing.

Additional ways to discourage prejudice are modeling, sharing, discouraging prejudicial comments, and supporting open, positive discussion among all students.

LESSON 17

Examining Prejudice

TARGETED EMOTIONAL DOMAINS Self-Awareness, Managing Emotions, Empathy, Handling Relationships

TARGETED INTELLIGENCES Verbal/Linguistic, Visual/Spatial, Bodily/Kinesthetic, Logical/Mathematical, Intrapersonal, Interpersonal

CURRICULAR AREAS Health, Language Arts, Social Studies, Math

▶ Activity 1: READ "NEW FRIENDS"

1. Explain to students that you want them to hear a story so that, in a later activity, they can use it to think about an important concept called *prejudice*.

2. Read the story, titled "New Friends," aloud, have students read it aloud, or have them read it to themselves.

NEW FRIENDS

Part One   STORY

Once upon a time there was a farm that was home to a community of horses. There were no cows, dogs, chickens, or rabbits, just horses. They liked it that way. All the horses lived, ate, worked, and played together happily. They did things in the same way, spoke the same language, and looked a lot alike. Every horse knew what to expect of every other horse. The farm was running smoothly, and the horses were very content. Until one day, when everything changed.

It was a quiet, sunny afternoon, and the horses were nibbling lazily on some hay just outside their stalls. One of the horses heard an unusual sound coming from behind the barn and trotted around to see what was happening. He couldn't believe what his eyes beheld! Standing in front of him were creatures the likes of which he had never seen! They looked a little like him and the other horses, except that jutting out of the middle of each of their foreheads was a long, pointed, shiny horn!

"How strange," he thought. "What are they? They're so different than we are." He ran around the back of the barn to tell the other horses what he had seen. "You won't believe what I just saw. There are strange creatures on the other side of the barn with long, pointed, shiny horns coming out of their heads. I've never seen anything like it!" he said. The parents gathered their colts and fillies close to them, saying, "Don't get too near those creatures. They are not like us. We do not know what kind of harm they may cause us. We must stay with our own kind."

The horses went about their business, watching the strange creatures with a mixture of curiosity and fear. Several of the horses gathered in groups, whispering. "They talk strangely, they look odd. I wonder if they eat what we eat, sleep like we sleep, feel the same things that we feel," said one horse. "Oh, probably not," another whispered. "I'm sure they have their own strange ways of doing everything." A third exclaimed, "I don't trust them! They might bring us problems or be dangerous. We should stick to our own kind. Work, eat, and play with our own kind. After all, we're probably better than they are and we just wouldn't mix."

The horned animals gathered in a group of their own behind the barn. "We must stay together," said one. "I don't like being away from the rest of our kind. I don't feel safe here. Who knows what harm may come to us?" "I don't know what these creatures are like," said another. "They talk strangely, they look odd. No horn. Imagine!"

As several of the horned animals continued to talk behind the barn one of the young animals drifted around to the side of the barn watching the horses with great curiosity. She wanted to find out for herself just what these creatures were like. They didn't seem all that fearsome to her, but it was hard not to be frightened by what everybody told her. As she watched, she couldn't help but notice how very much the horses looked like she did. She watched them eating. They ate a slightly different brand of hay, but it was still hay, nonetheless. They even played similar kinds of games, except the horses didn't have horns to help them pick things up.

As the young animal continued to watch the horses, she noticed that one of the little ones was looking in her direction. She didn't know whether to run away out of fear or move closer out of curiosity. Both animals thought, "Mom and Dad and everyone else has told me over and over again to stay away from those creatures, but I don't know. She just doesn't seem fearsome to me. I want to find out what she's like."

Both animals moved closer and closer to each other until they were just a few feet apart. Neither knew what to say. They stood that way for a few moments, each looking closely at the other, ready to gallop away if need be. Then, both at the same time blurted out a timid "hello." This made them both break out into a big smile and a giggle. They both knew, right then and there, that no creature that could smile like that could be all that bad.

They spent the next half hour speaking without stopping, asking questions of each other and answering each other, until curiosity was satisfied. "What do you eat? How do you sleep? Where do you come from? What is it like to have a horn? What is it like without one? How do you wash it?" As they talked, they slowly walked around the farm, barely noticing how far into the apple orchard they had drifted.

Part Two

Meanwhile, back at the farm, dinner time was fast approaching. As one of the horses was preparing the hay for the evening meal, she noticed that she hadn't seen her little filly in some time. She called to her, but received no reply. Concerned, she called the other horses around. "My little one is missing. I've been very worried with those strange creatures around. Who knows what might have happened to her!" A similar scene was taking place in the horned animals' stalls. "I knew we should have stayed where we were, with our own kind. I was afraid something like this was going to happen. We must go look for our little girl before it's too late! I say that we check the horses' stalls."

And with that, the horned animals took off around the barn at exactly the same time that the horses were coming toward them. A chorus of voices was heard: "I knew you shouldn't be trusted. What did you do with my little one? Where is she?" All of a sudden, the animals realized that there were two creatures missing. "You mean, one of your own is missing, too?" "Yes, indeed," replied one of the horses. "Then you had nothing to do with our baby being missing," said a horned one, and the horse said, "And you had nothing to do with our little one being gone." "What are we going to do?" asked another horse. "We have to find our little one." "We have to find our little one as well," replied the horned creature. "I believe that two heads and a horn are better than one. We may have better luck if we search together. We always have our horns to dig or to poke holes with, should we need them." "Yes, we must put our differences aside for the sake of the missing children."

And with that, the horses and the horned creatures set out to find the missing youngsters. Little did they know that at that very moment, the two young animals were making their way back toward the barn, talking nonstop. "I've really had fun with you," said the filly. "So did I," said the horned animal, which the filly now knew was called a unicorn. "Why is it that horses want to stay with horses and unicorns want to stay with unicorns?" asked the filly. "We make up all kinds of horrible things about each other, but we almost never talk to find out the truth. I'm so glad I've found a new friend and learned all kinds of things that I didn't know before." "I'm glad too. I think we should let everyone know what we've found . . ." But before the little unicorn could finish her last sentence, she and the filly realized that they were horn to horn and head to head with the entire community of horses and unicorns!

Every parent, unicorn and horse alike, began to talk at once. "Where were you? We were so worried. Don't you know you're not to wander off alone like that. Are you O.K.?" Just as quickly as it began, all the talking stopped as the horses and unicorns looked at each other with big smiles on their faces. "Do you realize that we sound exactly alike? We say the same things to our children, feel the same way about their safety. It doesn't seem to matter if we are horse or unicorn. The important things stay the same."

The pony and young unicorn looked at each other knowingly and eagerly began sharing with the rest of the community all they had learned about each other. That evening, for the first time on the farm, a new community was formed, of horses and unicorns together. Hay was shared, conversation was lively, and in the air was the wonderful excitement that comes from knowing that you have found new friends.

▶ Activity 2: INQUIRY

1. Prepare the Prejudice Check form by using the three column format (see Blacklines). Write the title at the top of the page. Label the columns *Day, Differences,* and *Whole Person.* Add the direction: "Fill in the day and mark under 'Differences' if you paid closest attention another person's differences that day, or mark under 'Whole Person' if you paid closest attention to all the qualities of another person that day."

2. Ask students to complete the inquiry sentence—"A time I believed I was better than someone else was . . . ." on the Prejudice handout (see Blacklines).

3. Introduce the Prejudice Check form and ask students to fill it out during the week.

▶ Activity 3: SCENE INVESTIGATION: NEW FRIENDS

1. Explain that the story "New Friends" from Activity 1, will be the basis of an investigation of the assumption:

THE ASSUMPTION

> "If someone is different than me,
> he or she is not as good a person as I am."

2. Develop a scene: The situation, setting, characters, and story line with ideas for dialogue are provided by the story.

PREPARE ROLES TO REFLECT ASSUMPTION

Thoughts

—When the horses first saw the unicorns, what were some of their thoughts about them? Example: They may cause us harm, we're better than they are.

—When the unicorns first saw the horses, what were some of their thoughts about them? Example: It's not safe, they're strange.

Feelings

—What do you think the horses and unicorns felt when they were near one another? Example: fear, mistrust, curiosity.

Behaviors

—How did the assumption, and the thoughts and feelings that followed, lead the animals to behave? Example: whispering, gossiping, staying away from one another.

3. Enact the scene: The students act out Part One of the story. It can be enacted in any way that they find most comfortable. For example, the story can be read aloud while students act out the movements. Or one student can narrate the story, stopping at key points to allow other students to act out those parts of the story. Or you can have the students enact the story using their own dialogue and gestures.

4. Reflect on the enactment:

Part Two seems to show a change of assumption. Ask students how, at the end of the story, the animals might have changed their initial assumption. For example, they might think, "If someone is different than me, he or she is just as good a person as I am." Ask these questions:

—When the two young animals met, what did they find out about one another? Example: that they were both friendly, that they were more alike than they thought.

—When the older animals found their youngsters, what did they find out about one another? Example: that neither was at fault for the youngsters' disappearance, that they all cared about their youngsters, that they were more alike than they thought.

5. Have students act out Part Two of the story, using their own dialogue if possible.

The story used was about animals and prejudice. Ask students to think about these questions: In what ways do humans make the same assumptions? What kinds of differences among people make us uncomfortable? What kinds of things to we feel when someone is different than us? What kinds of things do we do? What can we do to act based on the provable belief rather than the assumption?

REFLECTIVE
DETECTIVE

Another good follow-up activity is to have students create and illustrate a story of their own that shows the coming together of two different kinds of creatures or people.

About a week after the lesson, give students the opportunity to share highlights from their handouts and to discuss their experiences with prejudice during the week.

Primary Grade Modifications

READ "NEW FRIENDS"—Read the story aloud.

SCENE INVESTIGATION—Reread the sections of the story that will provide the answers to the questions.

REFLECTIVE DETECTIVE—Have students narrate and illustrate a story rather than write it out.

Middle and High School Modifications

READ "NEW FRIENDS"—Inform students that the story is the basis of a later activity. Have them read it silently.

SCENE INVESTIGATION—Divide students into groups. Have each group create a lesson for younger students based on the story. Have groups develop an introduction, make a choice as to whether they will enact the story or have the younger students do the acting, decide on which assumption the story is based and how to change that to a provable belief, and make analogies between the story and real-life situations. Feel free to fill in the gaps for them with the material provided in the lesson. As a closure activity, either have them lead a lesson in your class or with a lower grade.

PART III

Choosing to
ACT SENSIBLY

CHAPTER 5

Developing Emotional Intelligence Through

SKILL BUILDING

The lessons in this chapter address the skills necessary to execute increasingly effective life choices. One may know that one can choose to be an effective friend or family member, but if a person does not have the skills to execute this choice, it becomes merely a cognitive exercise. Communication skills in areas such as negotiating and listening help one apply emotional intelligence to improving a variety of relationships.

SkyLight Training and Publishing Inc.

LOOKING AT MANIPULATION

Sometimes, some people choose to try to get others to pay attention to them and to get other things they want in indirect ways. This is known as *manipulation*. Some examples of manipulation, such as whining and threatening, were explored in earlier activities. When manipulating, people try to get others to pay attention to them and to get other things they want by using their bodies and voices and choosing certain kinds of behaviors. But success is not guaranteed by using manipulative behavior. In addition, manipulating others often leads to misunderstanding and conflicts. Certain skills, such as stating one's feelings and asking directly for what one wants, can help to let others know more clearly what is desired. This increases the likelihood of achieving a goal and decreases the likelihood of misunderstanding and conflicts.

Lesson 18 addresses the issue of manipulation, helping students to look at helpful and less helpful methods of communication. Activity 1 provides an opportunity to reinforce cooperation. Activity 2 offers practice in the students' choice of relaxation techniques. Activity 3 builds students' awareness and understanding of manipulating actions. Activity 4 offers a kinesthetic exploration into a variety of methods of manipulation. Activity 5 offers an opportunity to rehearse effective communication techniques.

Additional ways to promote effective communication are modeling, reinforcing positive examples, and offering students a chance to reword ineffective communication techniques as they are observed.

LESSON 18

Looking at Manipulation

TARGETED EMOTIONAL DOMAINS Self-Awareness, Managing Emotions, Self-Control, Empathy, Handling Relationships

TARGETED INTELLIGENCES Verbal/Linguistic, Visual/Spatial, Logical/Mathematical, Bodily/Kinesthetic, Intrapersonal, Interpersonal

CURRICULAR AREAS Health, Social Studies, Language Arts, Math

▶ Activity 1: PULSE

1. Have the students sit in a circle, and join them.

2. Explain that you want them to hold hands with the people to either side of them. You begin by gently squeezing the hand of the person to your right. As soon as that student feels the "pulse," he or she immediately and gently squeezes the hand of the person to his or her right. This continues all the way around the circle. The purpose is to see how quickly the circle can pass the pulse around the room.

3. Ask students what helped to pass the pulse quickly. What stopped the pulse? What could they do to pass the pulse around the room with more speed?

▶ Activity 2: RELAXATION OF CHOICE

Have the students take a vote to determine which relaxation exercise to do, and do the exercise. Consider asking one of the students to lead the class in the exercise, with your guidance if it is needed. Remind students of the different relaxation exercises: rags, slow breathing, and tense/relax.

▶ Activity 3: INQUIRY

Give students the Manipulation Check form (see Blacklines), and ask them to fill it out during the week.

▶ Activity 4: MANIPULATION CIRCLE

1. Explain that most people use their bodies and voices in certain ways and choose certain kinds of behaviors in order to try to get others to pay attention to them and to get other things they want.

2. Tell students that you are going to describe a certain kind of behavior and give an example of that behavior. After each description, they are to come up with another example of that behavior and then show that behavior with their bodies and voices. As you go through the list of behaviors, students may add other manipulating behaviors that they or others choose to try. See Figure 5.1 for suggestions of manipulating behaviors to use for this activity.

MANIPULATION BEHAVIORS

Whining—"Nobody ever listens to me."

Acting out—"I'll run around the room until somebody pays attention to me."

Commanding—"Give me that now!"

Threatening—"You'd better give me that, or else!"

Accusing—"You never give me anything."

Labeling—"You're so mean."

Figure 5.1

3. Ask students how they feel when someone is whining, acting out, threatening, commanding, accusing, or labeling. Are they more or less likely to give that person what he or she wants? Do they use any of these behaviors to try to get what they want? How do others react when they do this?

▶ Activity 5: ASKING PRACTICE

1. Divide the students into groups of three. If students have difficulties working on their own, consider having several groups of three take turns demonstrating the skills for the rest of the class.

2. Tell students that they are going to practice the skills of stating their feelings and asking directly for what they want. When they state their feeling, they are to use a feeling word to help the other person understand how they feel. An example of stating their feeling would be, "I feel frustrated when I can't get anyone's attention." When stating their feeling, they do not accuse the other person of causing them to feel that way. They are merely explaining how they feel.

   Tell them that when they ask directly for what they want, they simply ask specifically for what they want. An example of asking directly would be "I'd like you to pay attention to me." When they ask directly, they do not demand that the other person give them what they want, but are merely asking for what they want. Give students the Asking Directly handout (see Blacklines), and ask them to complete the assertive statements on the form.

3. Tell them that they are going to practice these skills in groups of three. One student, the asker, asks for something; the partner is the person receiving the request; and the third student, the observer, observes the interaction.

4. The asker chooses something he or she wants from the partner. For example, he or she might want attention, a compliment, or some help with homework. The asker states his or her feeling about what is wanted and asks directly for it.

5. The partner lets the asker know how he or she felt about being asked for something in this way and lets the asker know that the partner would be likely to give the asker what was wanted, based on being asked in this way.

6. The observer closely watches the conversation, paying attention to use of body, voice, and the words being spoken by both participants. The observer shares his or her observations with the other two, letting them know how the new skills worked.

REFLECTIVE DETECTIVE

Have students add to their journals their observations, assumptions, beliefs, feelings, skills, and behaviors. Students may keep their journals using one or a variety of methods: stories, poetry, recipes, formulas, survival guides, drawings, songs, or any other ideas they may have.

About one week after this lesson, give students the opportunity to share highlights from their handouts and to discuss their experiences with asking directly for what they want.

Primary Grade Modifications

ASKING PRACTICE—Have several students demonstrate in front of the rest of the class rather than in small groups.

REFLECTIVE DETECTIVE—Try limiting their options to those they are capable of accomplishing.

Middle and High School Modifications

No modifications needed.

STRENGTHENING ACTIVE LISTENING AND FEEDBACK SKILLS

As shown in the previous lesson, people spend a great deal of time communicating with others around them. They use words and body language to get their ideas across, share feelings, and ask for what they want.

When communicating with someone, most people like to be listened to. Sometimes a person may think he or she has listened to another person and understands what that person is saying, but this is not always true. At times, when someone else is talking, some people become lost in their own thoughts and are not paying close attention to what is being said. Those thoughts may have nothing to do with what the speaker is saying. The listener may be thinking of a response to the speaker. Although trying to listen, if the listener disagrees with what is being said, he or she does not really hear what the speaker is trying to convey.

Certain skills, such as active listening and giving feedback, can help most people listen and communicate more effectively. *Active listening* uses the body to show another that one is paying attention to him or her. Repeating back what someone has said, called *giving feedback,* shows the speaker that the listener was listening. Figure 5.2 defines the behaviors of active listening and giving feedback.

LISTENING AND GIVING FEEDBACK DEFINITIONS

Active Listening—Using your body and face to let others know you are listening

Giving Feedback—Briefly repeating the facts of what others say without giving your own opinions or advice

---

Figure 5.2

When giving feedback, it is important that listeners repeat as closely as possible what was said and that they do not give their opinion about what was said or their advice about what to do about what was said; they simply restate the facts told to them.

Lesson 19 addresses the skills of listening and giving feedback. Activity 1 provides an opportunity to brainstorm and rehearse examples of listening body language. Activity 2 builds students' recognition and skill in listening and giving feedback through monitoring of their own activities. Activity 3 provides rehearsal in active listening. Activity 4 provides rehearsal in giving feedback

Additional opportunities for promoting active listening and giving feedback are modeling, reinforcing these skills as observed, and providing remedial opportunities for rehearsing these skills when necessary.

Strengthening Active Listening and Feedback Skills

LESSON 19

TARGETED EMOTIONAL DOMAINS Self-Awareness, Managing Emotions, Self-Control, Empathy, Handling Relationships

TARGETED INTELLIGENCES Verbal/Linguistic, Visual/Spatial, Logical/Mathematical, Bodily/Kinesthetic, Intrapersonal, Interpersonal

CURRICULAR AREAS Health, Social Studies, Language Arts, Math

▶ Activity 1: BRAINSTORM

1. Explain that the students are going to brainstorm as many ways as possible in which their bodies can show another person that they are listening. As they come up with an example, they all use their bodies to demonstrate that example. Some examples of behavior that show one is listening—leaning forward, making eye contact, nodding.

▶ Activity 2: LISTENING AND GIVING FEEDBACK CHECK

1. Prepare the Listening and Giving Feedback Check form by using the two column format (see Blacklines). Write the title at the top of the page. Label the columns *Day* and *Example*. Add the direction: "Fill in the day and describe a brief example of something you listened to someone say during that day."

2. Introduce the Listening and Giving Feedback Check form and ask students to complete it during the week.

▶ Activity 3: LISTENING PRACTICE

1. Divide the class into groups of three. If students have a difficult time working in small groups, choose three students to demonstrate this activity for the rest of the class. One student is the speaker; one, the listener; and one, the observer.

2. Explain to students that they are going to practice the skill of active listening, using their bodies to show that they are listening. (See Figure 5.2.)

3. The speaker speaks briefly about something that happened to him or her that week.

4. The listener uses his or her body to let the speaker know that he or she is being listened to. The listener can refer back to the brainstorm activity to remind him- or herself about the ways in which bodies can show that one is listening.

5. The observer watches the listener, looking to see the ways in which the listener is using his or her body to show that he or she is listening. The observer watches the speaker to see if the speaker is reacting in any way to being listened to in this manner.

6. Have the groups discuss among themselves what each person observed and felt.

METACOGNITIVE
DISCUSSION

What did students observe? How was the body used to show that they were listening? What was it like to listen in this way? Was it easier to pay attention to what was being said? What was it like to be listened to in this way? Did it make them want to tell their story more?

▶ Activity 4: FEEDBACK PRACTICE

1. Have the students stay in the same groups that they were in for Activity 3.

2. Explain that they are going to practice giving feedback. When giving feedback, a person is restating the facts that he or she has been given by the speaker, to let the speaker know that he or she has been heard (see Figure 5.2). For example, if the speaker said, "Last week, I forgot my tennis shoes for gym class," feedback from the listener might be, "You didn't have your tennis shoes in gym last week."

   Feedback does not give an opinion, such as, "You really shouldn't have forgotten your shoes," or give advice, such as, "Next time, you should leave your shoes by the front door." Feedback simply restates the facts as given.

3. As a warm-up, give students Feedback Practice (see Blacklines), and have them read the situation and choose the statement that is feedback.

4. The speaker speaks about the same situation as in Activity 3. The listener actively listens to the brief story and then gives the speaker feedback about what was heard. The observer listens to hear if the listener is giving feedback or giving opinion or advice. The listener also watches the speaker to observe reactions to the feedback. The group then discusses what each person observed and felt.

Ask students what they observed. Was it difficult or easy to give feedback about the facts and not give advice or opinions? Were they able to understand more or less of what was being said? What was it like to hear the feedback about what they said? Did they feel that they were heard?

METACOGNITIVE DISCUSSION

A good follow-up activity is to have students continue their journals. If they have been using one medium, add another as their method of journalizing. Remind them to add experiences from their most recent lessons on manipulating, asking for things directly, listening, and giving feedback.

About a week after this lesson, give students the opportunity to share highlights from their handouts and to discuss their experiences with listening and giving feedback during the week.

REFLECTIVE DETECTIVE

Primary Grade Modifications

BRAINSTORM—Give examples first.

LISTENING PRACTICE—Have several students demonstrate in front of the class rather than in small groups.

Middle and High School Modifications

No modifications needed.

DEVELOPING ASSERTIVE-NESS

There are times when some people choose not to ask for what they want because they do not feel that they have a right to do so. Or they may ask for what they want, but they do so using very little energy. By acting *passively*, they are telling others by what they say and how they say it that they really do not have a right to be asking and that they do not expect to receive what they are asking for.

At times, some people choose to demand what they want, using more energy than they need and imposing on others' rights, that is, acting *aggressively*.

There is a way to use just the right amount of energy to ask for what is wanted and to refuse what is not wanted. People can ask for things *assertively*, which acknowledges their rights but does not impose on others' rights. Acting in this way can help get what is wanted but avoid conflicts.

When someone is trying to get a person to do something that the person does not want to do or if a person is being physically threatened, an initial response might be to assertively deny the request. However, if pressure continues, a person may sometimes have to behave more aggressively to get the initiator to stop.

Lesson 20 explores and offers rehearsal in assertiveness, comparing it to passivity and aggression. Activity 1 offers a kinesthetic exploration of passivity, assertiveness, and aggressiveness. Activity 2 builds students' awareness of response choices that they can make. Activity 3 offers rehearsal in clear communication through tone of voice. Activity 4 provides an opportunity to practice and distinguish passive, aggressive, and assertive behaviors through brief scenes.

Additional ways to promote assertiveness are through modeling, rewarding assertive behaviors, and offering in-class opportunities to replay problematic situations using assertive behaviors.

LESSON 20

Developing Assertiveness

TARGETED EMOTIONAL DOMAINS   Self-Awareness, Managing Emotions, Self-Control, Empathy, Handling Relationships

TARGETED INTELLIGENCES   Verbal/Linguistic, Visual/Spatial, Logical/Mathematical, Bodily/Kinesthetic, Intrapersonal, Interpersonal

CURRICULAR AREAS   Health, Social Studies, Language Arts, Math

▶ Activity 1: PASSIVE/ASSERTIVE/AGGRESSIVE GREETINGS

1. Explain that this activity gives students the opportunity to practice using just the right amount of energy to say something.

2. Tell students that they will do this activity three times. In each case, after a count to three, they say the word *hello:* the first time, they say it passively; the second, assertively; and the third, aggressively. Each time, they are to use both their bodies and voices to express the kind of greeting they are giving.

3. Ask them to think about some of the differences in the ways they used their bodies and voices in each of the greetings. How did they feel as they experienced each greeting? Which kind of greeting made them the most comfortable?

▶ Activity 2: ASSERTIVENESS CHECK

1. Prepare the Assertiveness Check form by using the four column format (see Blacklines). Write the title at the top of the page. Label columns *Day, Passive, Aggressive,* and *Assertive.* Add the directions: "Fill in the day and mark under 'Passive' if you were mostly passive that day, 'Aggressive' if you were mostly aggressive that day, or 'Assertive' if you were mostly assertive that day."

2. Ask students to complete the assertive statements on the Assertiveness handout (see Blacklines).

3. Introduce the Assertiveness Check form to students and ask them to complete it during the week.

▶ Activity 3: YES/NO

1. Explain that the class is going to practice saying the words *yes* and *no* assertively and aggressively, expressing the way they are saying the words with their voices and facial expressions. On the count of three, all say the word *yes*. First, students say the word assertively, pretending for example, that they are saying the word as if their teacher had asked them if they wanted to try to solve the problem on the board and they wanted to try it.

2. The next time they say the word aggressively, that is, they are to say the word as if a classmate were trying over and over again to get them to smoke a cigarette and has now asked if they are sure they do not want to try just a puff. They are sure they do not want to try it and answer aggressively.

3. This time, on the count of three, all say the word *no*. First, they say the word assertively, as if they are being asked if they will show a classmate the answers to a test but do not think it is right and will not do so. Second, they say the word aggressively, as if a classmate is trying to force them to take a taste of beer and they are sure they do not want to try it.

4. Ask students in what specific ways their voice and facial expressions reflect the way they said the words. In what kinds of situations would it be most helpful to speak assertively? In what kinds of situations would it be most helpful to speak aggressively?

▶ Activity 4: ASSERTIVENESS PRACTICE

1. Explain that students are going to enact several brief scenes in order to practice assertive behaviors. First, they enact the scenes behaving passively and then, behaving aggressively. Then, they use their investigative know-how to change the scene so that they are behaving assertively. You can ask students for situations to enact and for behaviors and consequences resulting from each scenario.

2. Enact the first scene (for passive behavior): A book bag is taken by a classmate at recess. The student says nothing and stands there whimpering as the contents of his or her book bag are thrown around the playground.

3. Enact the second scene (for aggressive behavior): The student yells and pushes his or her classmate to the ground. This results in a fight for which both students are blamed and punished, and the book bag is kept by the teacher.

4. Enact the third scene (for assertive behavior): The student asks directly and firmly for his classmate to return his or her book bag. The classmate tries to upset the bag's owner by teasing and threatening, but the student does not respond to this and asks the classmate to return the book bag. Seeing that he or she is not going to get to the student, the classmate returns the book bag and walks away, grumbling.

REFLECTIVE
DETECTIVE

Students continue writing in their journals, adding media and experiences relating to the current lesson.

About a week after this lesson, give students the opportunity to share highlights from their handouts and to discuss their experiences with assertiveness during the past week.

Primary Grade Modifications

PASSIVE/ASSERTIVE/AGGRESSIVE GREETINGS—Demonstrate first.

YES/NO—Use different examples.

> Yes: For assertive, try "Our teacher has asked if we want to hear a story and we would like to hear it." For aggressive, try "A stranger asks us to come into their car for some candy. We know it's not safe to do this, and he asks us if we're sure we don't want any."

> No: For assertive, try "A friend asks if we are done with a toy that he wants and we are not done yet." For aggressive, try "Someone wants to touch us in a place we don't want them to touch."

ASSERTIVENESS PRACTICE—Replace the book bag with a toy.

Middle and High School Modifications

YES/NO—Use different examples.

> Yes: For assertive, try "Say the word as if you are being asked if you think you are a good person." For aggressive, try "Say yes as if someone was pushing you into a sexual relationship, and asking you if you were sure that you didn't want to get involved that way."

> No: For assertive, try "Say no as if you were being asked if you wanted a beer and you didn't want one." For aggressive, try "Say no as if someone was trying to harm you."

ASSERTIVENESS PRACTICE—Use different examples, such as being teased.

LEARNING COMMUNICATION AND NEGOTIATION

As discussed, when people communicate with each other, sometimes one person wants one thing and the other person wants something else. In situations like this, sometimes the participants choose to use methods of communication that lead to misunderstanding and arguments and result in neither getting what is wanted.

In order to avoid arguments and please all participants, some people use a method of communication called *negotiating* in which people work together to come up with a solution that is agreeable to everyone. The steps to successful negotiating are shown in brief form in Figure 5.3.

STEPS TO SUCCESSFUL NEGOTIATING

State desires directly

Give feedback

Brainstorm possible solutions

Agree on a solution and follow it through

Figure 5.3

To negotiate means doing the following:
- Each person in turn states directly what he or she wants without manipulating and without being interrupted.
- After a person states what he or she wants, the other person gives feedback to the requester, thus confirming that he or she has been heard. The feedback given is a restatement of facts and is not advice or opinions.
- Both people brainstorm to come up with solution alternatives. These solutions must be ones that take the desires of both people into consideration. Each person might not get exactly what is wanted, and each might have to give up something for both people to be satisfied. For example, if both wanted to play with the one ball left in the playground, one solution might be that both would play with the ball together. Each gives up the ability to play alone with the ball, but they both still are able to play with the ball. Another solution might be that each person plays with the ball for half of recess. Each person gives up half of the time with the ball, but both are able to play with it alone.
- Both people agree on a solution and follow it through.

Lesson 21 explores and rehearses the art and skill of negotiation. Activity 1 offers an opportunity to examine effective and ineffective communication methods. Activity 2 offers rehearsal in negotiation. Activity 3 builds negotiating awareness and skill by focusing on students' personal efforts.

Additional ways to support negotiation are to model it, to try to work together with students to make joint choices, and to offer students opportunities to work out conflicts through negotiation.

Learning Communication and Negotiation

TARGETED EMOTIONAL DOMAINS Self-Awareness, Managing Emotions, Self-Control, Empathy, Handling Relationships

TARGETED INTELLIGENCES Verbal/Linguistic, Visual/Spatial, Logical/Mathematical, Bodily/Kinesthetic, Intrapersonal, Interpersonal

CURRICULAR AREAS Health, Social Studies, Language Arts, Math

▶ Activity 1: BRAINSTORMING ABOUT COMMUNICATING AND NEGOTIATING

1. Explain that when someone wants one thing and another person wants something else, sometimes the two may behave in ways that lead to problems, although at other times they use positive methods of communicating that help them to figure out what to do.

2. The students are going to brainstorm a list of behaviors that might lead to problems in such situations and a list of behaviors that might help them to work out a solution.

3. First, have students develop a list of problems in communicating. Examples of problems include not listening, yelling, not being willing to compromise, and leaving.

4. Next, have students develop examples of solutions that might help them, including listening, talking calmly, being willing to compromise, and going over alternatives to arrive at a solution together.

▶ Activity 2: NEGOTIATING PRACTICE

1. Divide the class into groups of three. If students have a difficult time working in small groups, choose three students to demonstrate this activity for the rest of the class.

2. Explain that they are going to practice negotiating, following the four steps of the negotiating process. Introduce the four steps, using the material outlined in the lesson introduction. Also, see Figure 5.3.

3. When you are comfortable that the students understand the idea of negotiating, ask two students to be negotiators and one to be an observer.

4. The negotiators decide on something they will negotiate about. For example, both might want the same piece of cake, or one friend might want to play house but the other wants to watch television. Following the four step process, they are to negotiate a solution they both agree on.

5. The observer watches the negotiators, checking to see how the steps are followed. The observer checks how each person stated what they wanted, what the feedback was like, and how the solution was determined.

6. The group discusses what each person observed and felt.

METACOGNITIVE DISCUSSION

Did either negotiator use manipulation to get across what he or she wanted or were desires stated directly? Was the feedback based on the facts of what each person said or did it include advice or opinions? Were the brainstormed solutions fair to both people or did they reflect the needs of just one person? Was a decision reached by both people? What could have made the negotiating work even better? In what situations could students use this skill?

▶ Activity 3: NEGOTIATING CHECK

1. Prepare the Negotiating Check form by using the two column format (see Blacklines). Write the title at the top of the page. Label columns *Day* and *Example*. Add the directions: "Fill in the day and describe a brief example of a situation in which you negotiated to arrive at a solution."

2. Introduce the Negotiating Check form to students and ask them to fill it out during the week.

REFLECTIVE DETECTIVE

Have students continue writing in their journals, adding media and experiences relating to this lesson.

About one week after this lesson, give students the opportunity to share highlights from their handouts and to discuss their experiences with negotiating during the week.

Primary Grade Modifications

BRAINSTORMING ABOUT COMMUNICATING AND NEGOTIATING—Give examples first. Or give students two lists and have them determine which one would help with solutions and which would be problematic.

NEGOTIATING PRACTICE—Enact the negotiating steps as you describe them. Have one group do this in front of the class under your close direction.

Middle and High School Modifications

NEGOTIATING PRACTICE—Offer a different example, such as negotiating a curfew with a parent.

BUILDING STUDY SKILLS

In this lesson, success and pride are discussed with the students, and skills are suggested with which to achieve both. Most people like to succeed, take pride in what they do, and want to feel good about themselves. School work is one area in which students can all succeed and take pride. The more effort that is put into work, the more that can be achieved.

Sometimes, however, some students may feel that, despite their hardest efforts, they are not doing as well as they would like. Sometimes they may assume that their only choice is to stop trying and give up.

In spite of holding this feeling, students may still succeed. There are certain skills that, when learned, can help them succeed at a higher level.

Organizing desks and materials helps many people get needed objects with greater ease and speed, which frees more time for work. Directions help those who follow them to know exactly what to do and in what order to do it. Making an outline of what has been said in class helps many listeners identify the most important parts of what is being said. Making a summary of what is read helps many readers attend to the most important parts of the reading. Finding a special place and time for doing homework and rewarding themselves when they have done it helps many successful learners complete their homework regularly.

Lesson 22 examines and provides practice in study skills critical to students' success in school. Activity 1 provides practice with relaxation techniques. Activity 2 offers an opportunity to brainstorm effective school behaviors. Activity 3 provides practice in the study skills previously mentioned. Activity 4 builds students' awareness of the value of study skills by self-monitoring of their study efforts and results.

Additional opportunities for rehearsing skills such as following directions, outlining, and summarizing can be incorporated in daily activities. Desk organizing can also be encouraged. In addition, talk to students about their study habits at home and help them become more efficient.

LESSON 22

Building Study Skills

TARGETED EMOTIONAL DOMAINS   Self-Awareness, Managing Emotions, Self-Control

TARGETED INTELLIGENCES   Verbal/Linguistic, Visual/Spatial, Logical/Mathematical, Bodily/Kinesthetic, Intrapersonal, Interpersonal

CURRICULAR AREAS   Health, Social Studies, Language Arts, Math

▶ Activity 1: RELAXATION EXERCISE

Have the students vote on a relaxation exercise of their choice and do the exercise. Ask one of the students to lead the class in the exercise.

Ask students what their level of relaxation is now as compared with the beginning of the choice-making training. What has helped them most to relax? What effect does their level of relaxation have on their thoughts, feelings, and behaviors? What effect does their level of relaxation have on their ability to do well in school? Is it helpful to relax before doing an assignment or taking a test? How is it helpful?

METACOGNITIVE
DISCUSSION

▶ Activity 2: BRAINSTORMING ABOUT STUDYING

Ask students to brainstorm activities they think they could do that might help them perform better in school. These may be in-class as well as at-home activities. For example, the following might be included

—following directions

—finding a special place and time for doing homework.

▶ Activity 3: STUDY PRACTICE

1. Tell students that they are going to practice each study skill individually.

2. Explain that you are going to give them directions as to exactly what they are going to do and in what order they are going to do it. Following these directions is their first study skill to practice! After hearing the directions, students are to begin acting on the first direction given.

3. The first direction is that they are to write an outline of the directions that you give them. In the outline, they are to number the directions in the order they are to be done. After each number, they are to write one or two words that would describe each particular direction, for example "1. Organize desk. "

4. The second direction is to organize their desks and materials. They are to look at what they have in and on their desks and throw out what they do not need. Then, they are to find specific places for the things that they do use and put their things in those places, where they will always be put.

5. The third direction is to ask each student to choose a brief story and read it quietly. They are to write a brief summary of what they read. The summary is to describe the main points of the story in a few sentences.

6. The fourth direction is that you are giving them a brief assignment to complete at home. (Give the students an assignment of your choice.) They are to choose a specific place to complete the assignment. The place is to be one in which they would find it best to do their homework. A quiet place without distractions might be helpful. They are to choose a specific time to do their assignment. The time is one that they would find best for doing their homework. It might be helpful to do the assignment not too long after they get home, before other activities get in the way. They are to choose a specific reward for themselves, to be enjoyed after they complete the assignment. An example of a reward might be an hour of watching television or a special snack.

▶ Activity 4: INQUIRY

1. Ask students to complete the study skills sentence—"One skill that could help me do better in school is . . . ." on the Study Skills handout (see Blacklines).

2. Give students the Study Skills Check (see Blacklines) and ask them to fill it out during the week.

REFLECTIVE DETECTIVE   Students continue writing in their journals, adding media and experiences relating to the current lesson.

About one week after this lesson, ask students to share highlights from their handouts and discuss their experiences in using study skills with each other.

Primary Grade Modifications

BRAINSTORMING ABOUT STUDYING—Give examples first.

STUDY PRACTICE—Draw or storyboard the directions, rather than write the outline and summary. Also, read a story aloud.

Middle and High School Modifications

REFLECTIVE DETECTIVE—Discuss assumptions that might get in the way of good study habits and scholastic achievement, such as "I must be perfect."

CLARIFYING VALUES AND CONSEQUENCES

As discussed in the first part, when someone makes a choice, that person is deciding what is best between two or more alternatives. When choosing, it is helpful to know the things that are truly most important to the chooser, in other words, the chooser's *values*. In this way, a person can choose in accordance with those values.

It is not only helpful to consider values when choosing between alternatives but also it is helpful to consider what may happen as a result of those choices, in other words, the *consequences* of choosing. When people consider the possible consequences of their choices, they can choose whether they are willing to accept those consequences. They can then choose whether they truly want to make that choice.

Sometimes, there are difficulties in making choices based on values. Difficulties that arise include having to wait to get something that is really wanted or giving it up entirely if a person is unwilling to accept the consequences of the choice.

At times, choices between values must be made as well. For example, let's say that someone values being a nice person and also values doing well in school. This person is using the classroom computer for an important assignment during his or her turn, but a classmate, who is behind in his or her work, asks to use the computer. Now the student must decide between continuing on the computer or letting the classmate use it, which is really making a choice between working on school success or working on being nice to someone.

Lesson 23 offers an opportunity to examine the values underlying choices and the consequences of basing choices on those values. Activity 1 offers an additional experience in cooperation. Activity 2 provides an opportunity for students to rank values in order of their importance to them. Activity 3 provides an opportunity for students to closely examine the consequences they would be willing to accept for a choice they might make. Activity 4 builds awareness of personal values and behavior, including a look at consequences of a choice.

Additional ways to help students examine their values and the consequences of their choices would be to discuss the values upon which students' observed choices are based as well as pointing out and examining possible and real consequences of choices made.

LESSON 23

Clarifying Values and Consequences

TARGETED EMOTIONAL DOMAINS Self-Awareness, Managing Emotions, Self-Control, Empathy, Handling Relationships

TARGETED INTELLIGENCES Verbal/Linguistic, Visual/Spatial, Logical/Mathematical, Bodily/Kinesthetic, Intrapersonal, Interpersonal

CURRICULAR AREAS Health, Social Studies, Language Arts, Math

▶ Activity 1: GROUP ACTIVITY

Have the students vote on a group exercise of their choice, such as Alphabet or Pulse, and do the exercise.

METACOGNITIVE DISCUSSION

Ask students to consider how they chose to complete the exercise. Did they choose to use what they know about what makes cooperation work? Was the exercise easier than at the beginning of the choice-making training or more difficult? How do their choices about cooperation affect them in their daily lives? What new choices are they now making regarding cooperation?

▶ Activity 2: VALUES RANKING

1. Explain that students are going to identify and rank values in this activity.

2. Tell them that you are going to list a number of values. As each value is listed, they are to write it on their paper. There are no right or wrong answers, only their own answers. Examples of values that might be used are success, popularity, money, happiness, family harmony, feeling good about yourself, and being the kind of person you want to be.

3. After students have listed all the values, have them put the number one next to the value that is most important to them and continue numbering each of the values in the order of declining importance.

METACOGNITIVE DISCUSSION

Ask if it was easy to order their values. What made it difficult? Did everyone find the same values to be of equal importance? Where do values come from? Does one ever change values? When might that be?

▶ Activity 3: ACTION-CONSEQUENCE CONTINUUM

1. Explain that students are going to examine several values. They will look at several consequences that might occur as a result of making a variety of choices in accordance with those values. They are to determine which consequences they would be willing to accept, and therefore, which choice they would be more likely to make.

2. Tell them that you will announce a value, identify actions that one might take in order to act in accordance with that particular value, and describe the possible consequences of taking that action. Explain that you are going to describe a number of action–consequence pairs that are related but become increasingly different from each other. Remind students to listen carefully to each action–consequence pair and be thinking if they would vote for it.

3. First, read all the action–consequence pairs for one value. Then give students the opportunity to vote for their choices by calling out each pair. Examples of values, actions, and consequences include

Value: Success

Action–consequence pair 1: In order to achieve success, students might choose to pick a particular place and time to do their homework and do it at that time and place every day. They would do this even when there was a program that they really wanted to watch on television or a friend they really wanted to be with at that time. The consequence of this choice might be that they would miss good television shows and some fun times with their friends but that they would get better and better grades.

Action–consequence pair 2: Students might choose a place and time to do their homework, and do it sometimes at that time and place. However, if a friend called and wanted to go somewhere, they would leave and not do their homework that day. The consequence of this choice might be that they would enjoy more time with their friend but that their grades would go up and down.

Action–consequence pair 3: Students might choose to never do homework and rely on luck to get by. On a day when they were not sure of their good luck, they might choose, just this once, to look on someone else's test for the answers. The consequence of this choice might be that on this particular day they might get an A on that one test. They might also wonder if they could ever get good grades on their own. They might also have a difficult time achieving the value of feeling good about themselves, believing that cheating is not right. They might be torn between the values of achieving success and feeling good about themselves.

Action–consequence pair 4: Students may choose to look on someone else's paper all the time. Because they have not done the work in the past, they doubt their capabilities. The consequence of this choice might be that they would find it more and more difficult not to get caught. They might feel worse and worse about themselves and their achievements, and they might understand less and less in class.

Value: Happiness

Action–consequence pair 1: In order to be happier, students may choose to think positive thoughts and get involved with things that they enjoy. The consequence of this choice might be that they would have to work hard to change old emotional habits but that they would be able to be happier whenever they chose to be happier.

Action–consequence pair 2: In order to be happier, students may choose to do nothing. The consequence of this choice might be that they would not have to work hard to change old emotional habits and that they could do what they have always done, but they would remain unhappy a lot of the time.

Action–consequence pair 3: In order to be happier, students may choose, just one time, to drink alcohol or use another drug. The consequence of this choice might be that they would feel good at first, but then they would become sick, and they would feel unhappy again. Or they might find that they begin to want more and more alcohol or drug to help them feel happier.

Action–consequence pair 4: In order to be happier, students may choose to always drink alcohol or take drugs. The consequence of this choice might be that the drugs or alcohol might help them to feel happier at first but would quickly start to make them feel unhappy, and that they no longer had a choice about whether to take them. Their body would have a physical urge for them, and they would hurt if they stopped taking them. Also, they might find it harder and harder to do their schoolwork, making it more difficult for them to achieve the value of success.

Value: Money

Action–consequence pair 1: In order to have money, students might choose to do what they could to earn it, such as working on a paper route, baby-sitting, or doing odd jobs for their neighbors. The consequence of this choice might be that they would have less time for recreation but that they would feel a sense of achievement and enjoy having their own money, to do with what they liked.

Action–consequence pair 2: In order to have money, they might choose to ask their parents for money all the time. The consequence of this choice might be that they would have more time for recreation but that they would not always be able to count on having money, and they might run into difficulties with their parents.

Action–consequence pair 3: In order to have money, they might choose to take just a little money from their parents' wallets, just one time, promising themselves that they will return it as soon as they can. The consequence of this choice might be that they would have some money without giving up any recreation time, but that they would feel bad, worry about getting caught, or actually get into trouble.

Action–consequence pair 4: In order to have money, they might choose to steal from others all the time. The consequence of this choice might be that they would have some money without having to work but that they would eventually be sent to jail. Even if they tried to make money a different way, if they got out of jail, they would have no skills with which to earn money, so they might have to go back to prison.

▶ Activity 4: CLARIFYING VALUES AND CONSEQUENCES PRACTICE

1. Prepare the Values and Consequences Check form by using the four column format (see Blacklines). Write the title at the top of the page. Label columns *Day, Choice, Value,* and *Consequence.* Add directions: "Fill in the day, a choice you made, the value it was based on, and the consequences of that choice."

2. Ask students to complete the matching exercise on the Clarifying Values and Consequences handout (see Blacklines).

3. Give students the Values and Consequences Check form and ask them to complete it during the week.

Students continue adding media and experiences relating to the current lesson to their journals.

About one week after this lesson, give students the opportunity to share highlights from their handouts and to discuss the choices they made that week, the values upon which the choices were based, and the consequences that occurred as a result of their choices.

REFLECTIVE
DETECTIVE

Primary Grade Modifications

GROUP ACTIVITY—Remind students of the options by doing a portion of the exercises.

VALUES RANKING—Define terms such as success and popularity. If students cannot write, have them do this in the form of the "barometer," standing on the end of the barometer that would represent their highest value.

ACTION–CONSEQUENCE CONTINUUM—Offer different examples where appropriate.

Middle and High School Modifications

REFLECTIVE DETECTIVE—Discuss the difficulty with acting according to one's own values when those values are in conflict with those of the majority.

CHAPTER 6

Developing Emotional Intelligence Through

SELF-CONTROL

The three lessons in this chapter help students apply their emotional intelligence and choice-making skills to problem solving and gaining self-control. Students are going to examine three difficult choices (cheating, stealing, and abusing alcohol and other drugs) that they may encounter. First, they look at the assumptions and facts related to each particular choice. Then, they explore what may happen in the present and in the future if these choices are made.

INVESTIGATING CHEATING

Cheating, defined as "to fool by trickery," is seen as behavior that seems to be based, at least partly, on the assumption "I don't have to work hard at school. I'll be lucky and win the lottery or become famous." But the facts show that cheating does not solve all problems and that the consequences of being caught are long lasting. See Figure 6.1 for information about cheating.

CHEATING FACTS

- Definition—Cheat: to fool by trickery.
- Assumption—I don't have to work hard at school. I'll be lucky and win the lottery or become famous.
- Belief—It is important to work hard in school.

Facts

- One of five adults cannot read or write.
- Many people cannot read warning labels, order from a menu, or fill out job applications.
- There is a 40% high school dropout rate.
- The difference in lifetime earnings between someone who has stayed in school and someone who has dropped out of school is hundreds of thousands of dollars.

Figure 6.1

Lesson 24 helps students examine the choice of cheating. Activity 1 has students exploring personal experiences with cheating. Activity 2 explores the choice of cheating through the development, enactment, and analysis of two brief scenes, one that depicts the effect of cheating on the present life of the individual making this choice and the second that depicts the effect that this choice might have on that person's future.

Should a student be observed making the choice to cheat, it might be helpful to have him or her examine his or her choice, assumptions, and future consequences of his or her actions.

Investigating Cheating

TARGETED EMOTIONAL DOMAINS Self-Awareness, Managing Emotions, Self-Control, Empathy, Handling Relationships

TARGETED INTELLIGENCES Verbal/Linguistic, Visual/Spatial, Logical/Mathematical, Bodily/Kinesthetic, Intrapersonal, Interpersonal

CURRICULAR AREAS Health, Social Studies, Language Arts, Math

▶ Activity 1: INQUIRY

Ask students to complete the sentence "An experience I had with cheating was when . . . ." (There is no handout.)

▶ Activity 2: SCENE INVESTIGATION: CHEATING CONSEQUENCES

1. Tell students that they are to develop and enact two brief scenes. The difficult choice to be enacted is the choice of cheating. The first scene depicts the difficult choice being made and the effect that this has on the present life of the individual making this choice. The second scene depicts the effect that this choice has on the future life of this individual. For convenience, two possible scenes are outlined briefly. Feel free to embellish these outlines or develop an original scene based on ideas from students.

2. Share the two scene outlines with the students. Encourage them to create their own dialogue and actions to go with a scene.

CHEATING CONSEQUENCES SCENES

Scene 1

As a young person, Pam often pretends that she is sick so that she can miss school. When she is in school, she rarely listens or pays attention. As an older student, Pam never does homework because she feels that she would not do the work as well as she would like. She gets by for a while on luck. A difficult test is given for which she has not studied, and Pam looks on a neighbor's paper for the answers. The teacher catches her and sends her to the office to discuss the matter with the principal. Pam tells the principal that she will never do it again. When the next test is given out, Pam does not trust her own knowledge and copies from a classmate again.

Scene 2

Pam is now in her twenties and has dropped out of high school, finding it more and more difficult. She has been applying for jobs and has not been hired for any of them. She is now applying for a job at McDonald's and cannot fill out the application because she does not understand some of the questions. Pam goes into the office to be interviewed. When asked why she did not finish filling out the application, she tries to bluff her way through it. However, the manager tells her that she is not McDonald's material and sends her out the door without a job.

3. Have students discuss the choice made. They are to use all of their choice-making skills to determine whether this was the best possible choice. Have them ask a series of questions related to making the choice. (Brief possible responses are shown.)

Was this choice based on assumptions or facts?

   —assumptions

On which assumptions was the choice based?

   —I don't have to work hard at school.

   —I must be perfect.

How could the assumptions be changed into provable beliefs?

   —It is important to work hard at school.

   —I do not have to be perfect.

What were the consequences of the choice?

   —being called into the principal's office

   —losing self-trust and developing a pattern of cheating

   —dropping out of school

   —having trouble finding a job

Would these consequences be acceptable to them?

   —no

Was the choice based on their highest value?

   —no

What might have been a better choice?

—doing the schoolwork as well as possible and asking for help when having difficulties

4. Ask students to rewrite the scenes to reflect what they feel would be the best possible choice, showing the effect of that choice on the present and future life of that individual.

Students continue adding comments and thoughts to their journals, using different media and experiences relating to the current lesson.

About one week after this lesson, give students the opportunity to discuss experiences—past, present, and future—with cheating.

REFLECTIVE DETECTIVE

Primary Grade Modifications

No modifications needed.

Middle and High School Modifications

No modifications needed.

INVESTIGATING STEALING

This lesson examines the choice of *stealing*, defined as "to take the property of another without right or permission." See Figure 6.2. for the assumptions and facts associated with stealing. The assumption that "I can take something from someone just once and that does not mean that I am a thief" is coupled with the assumption "I can never be happy and life will be awful unless certain things are a certain way" to create a dilemma that has affected many children under the age of eighteen.

STEALING FACTS

- Definition—Steal: to take the property of another without right or permission.

- Assumptions:

  I can take something from someone just once and that doesn't mean I'm a thief.

  I can never be happy and life will be awful unless certain things are a certain way.

Facts

- Many children under the age of 18 will commit some kind of crime for which they could be arrested.

- Juvenile criminals can be sent to jail as well as other public and private institutions.

Figure 6.2

Lesson 25 examines the choice of stealing. Activity 1 has students exploring personal experiences with stealing. Activity 2 explores the choice of stealing through the development, enactment, and analysis of two scenes. The first scene depicts the effect of stealing on the present life of the individual making this choice. The second scene depicts the effect that this choice might have on the future of the person making this choice.

Should a student be observed making the choice to steal, it might be helpful to have him or her examine his or her choice, assumptions, and future consequences of his or her actions.

Investigating Stealing

LESSON
25

TARGETED EMOTIONAL DOMAINS Self-Awareness, Managing Emotions, Self-Control, Empathy, Handling Relationships

TARGETED INTELLIGENCES Verbal/Linguistic, Visual/Spatial, Logical/Mathematical, Bodily/Kinesthetic, Intrapersonal, Interpersonal

CURRICULAR AREAS Health, Social Studies, Language Arts, Math

▶ Activity 1: INQUIRY

Ask students to write about "An experience I had with stealing was when . . . ." (There is no handout.)

▶ Activity 2: SCENE INVESTIGATION: STEALING CONSEQUENCES

1. Explain that students are to investigate two scenes about the choice and consequences of stealing. Share the following scenes with them to use as the basis of the investigation or develop appropriate scenes of your own.

STEALING
CONSEQUENCES
SCENES

Scene 1

A youngster, José, is at a toy store with a friend. He sees a toy car that he really wants, but he doesn't have enough money for it. He knows that he would be so happy if he could only have the car that he really wants. His friend suggests that he just take it because the store has a lot of them and would never miss the one that he took. José takes the car because he believes that he just can't be happy unless he has it right away. He is stopped by the store manager before he gets to the exit. The store manager calls José's parents. They come to the store and make their son return the item and promise to never steal anything again. The next time José is at a store, he takes a chocolate bar without paying for it. As a teenager, he sees money on his parents' dresser when they are not home. He wants to go to a movie and doesn't have his own money. Believing that his parents will never know and never miss the money, he takes it.

> **Scene 2**
>
> José is now in his forties and is in jail. He is in an office, trying to convince a panel of officials that he should be let out of jail on parole. He tells them that he promises never to steal another thing and that he will work very hard to be a model citizen. He leaves the room as the panel discusses whether to grant his parole. When he returns, the panel tells him that his parole is not going to be granted. Even though he may want to make different choices and change his ways, he has not shown that he is able to make this choice. Every time he has been released on parole, he has stolen again and been brought back to jail. Therefore, he will serve his entire sentence with no parole.

2. Have students discuss the controlling assumption. The following questions, with possible answers, are pertinent to the discussion:

Was this choice based on assumptions or facts?

　　—assumptions

On which assumptions was the choice based?

　　—I can take something from someone just once and that does not mean I am a thief.

　　—I can never be happy and life will be awful unless certain things are a certain way.

How could they rewrite the assumptions into provable beliefs?

　　—If I take something from someone, I am acting as a thief.

　　—I can be happy if I choose to be happy.

What were the consequences of the choice?

　　—getting into trouble with parents

　　—developing a pattern of stealing

　　—going to jail

　　—staying in jail for life

Would these consequences be acceptable to them?

　　—no

Was this choice based on their highest value?

　　—no

What might have been a better choice?

—asking parents to buy him the toy, trying to get a job to save money to buy it himself, playing with toys he already owns, asking his parents to borrow some money

3. Have students rewrite the scenes, using different assumptions.

Students continue adding comments and thoughts to their journals, using different media and experiences relating to the current lesson.

About one week after this lesson, give students the opportunity to discuss experiences—past, present, and future—with stealing.

REFLECTIVE
DETECTIVE

Primary Grade Modifications

No modifications needed.

Middle and High School Modifications

No modifications needed.

INVESTIGATING ABUSE OF ALCOHOL AND OTHER DRUGS

Lesson 26 examines the choice of using *alcohol,* defined as a drug found in drinks such as beer, wine, or liquor, and taking *drugs,* defined as chemicals that change the way the body and mind work. Figure 6.3 presents the assumptions and facts associated with alcohol and other drug use. Assumptions such as "I can take as much alcohol or other drugs as I want and they won't hurt me, and I can stop when I want to" and "I must give in to pressure to be cool and to be liked by everyone, or it would be awful" combine to produce a dangerous choice for some students.

Students need to know that there are some safe drugs that are prescribed when one is ill, but that there are other drugs that are harmful to minds and bodies. These drugs can cause people using them to be unable to stand or walk; make them pass out; cause damage to parts of their bodies, such as their liver, stomach, or brain; and cause many problems for themselves, their family, and their friends. Some people may become dependent on, or addicted to, a drug, taking it more and more and having difficulty in stopping.

The process of addiction is multistaged. At first, drugs are used because people believe it will take away their scary or sad feelings. They may learn that, although the drug does not take away the feeling for good, it may help them forget those feelings for a while. Following this, they may begin to look forward to using the drug and will actively look for it. Until this point, people are still able to choose other ways to make themselves feel better, besides using the drug. However, they are likely to choose the drug over any other method. Next, they have no choice except to take the drug because they need it to survive. Their body needs the chemicals and they ache if drugs are not taken. They use the drug on a regular basis because they have to. The final stage is one of three results: recovery, where very hard work with lots of help enable the person to stop taking the drug; serious illness; or death.

When youngsters use drugs, the drugs interfere with their growth; slow their learning; change their mood, causing anxiety, sadness, or anger; cause them problems in school and with friends and family; and leave them open to the process of addiction.

Activity 1 in this lesson has students exploring personal experiences with alcohol and other drug use. Activity 2 explores the choice of alcohol and other drug use through the development, enactment, and analysis of two scenes. The first scene depicts the effect of alcohol and other drug use on the present life of the individual making this choice. The second scene depicts the effect that this choice might have on the future of the person making this choice.

Should a student be observed making a choice to use alcohol and other drugs, it might be helpful to have him or her examine his or her choice, assumptions, and future consequences of his or her actions.

FACTS ABOUT ALCOHOL AND OTHER DRUGS

Definitions
- Alcohol—A drug found in drinks such as beer, wine, or liquor.
- Drug—A chemical that changes the way the body and mind work.
- Assumptions—I can take as much alcohol or other drugs as I want and they won't hurt me, and I can stop when I want to.
  —I must give in to pressure to be cool and to be liked by everyone, or it would be awful.
- Belief—I can be harmed by alcohol and other drugs, and eventually, I would not be able to stop when I wanted to stop.

Facts
- There are some drugs that are given to help us when we are sick.
- There are many drugs that harm our minds and bodies. These drugs may make us unable to stand or walk; cause us to pass out; cause damage to parts of our body, such as our liver, stomach, and brain; and cause many problems for us, our friends, and our families.
- When youngsters use drugs, drugs interfere with their growth; slow their learning; change their mood, causing stress, sadness, or anger; cause problems with school, friends, and family; and leave them open to the process of addiction.

Addiction Process
- People can become dependent on, or addicted to, a drug, making it more and more difficult to stop using the drug.
- At first, a person may use a drug to take away scary or sad feelings. People may learn that, although the drug doesn't take the feelings away for good, it may help them forget those feelings for a while.
- Next, a person may begin looking forward to using the drug and will actively look for the drug. Until this point, the person can still choose other ways to feel better, besides using the drug. However, he or she will choose the drug over any other method.
- Next, the person has no choice except to take the drug because he or she needs it to survive. His or her body needs the chemicals, and it hurts his or her body if the drug is not taken. The drug is used on a regular basis because the person has to.
- The final stage is either recovery, where the person works very hard with lots of help to stop taking the drug; serious illness; or death.

Figure 6.3

SkyLight Training and Publishing Inc.

LESSON 26

Investigating Abuse of Alcohol and Other Drugs

TARGETED EMOTIONAL DOMAINS Self-Awareness, Managing Emotions, Self-Control, Empathy, Handling Relationships

TARGETED INTELLIGENCES Verbal/Linguistic, Visual/Spatial, Logical/Mathematical, Bodily/Kinesthetic, Intrapersonal, Interpersonal

CURRICULAR AREAS Health, Social Studies, Language Arts, Math

▶ Activity 1: INQUIRY

Ask students to complete this sentence: "An experience I had with alcohol or other drugs was when . . . ." (There is no handout.)

▶ Activity 2: SCENE INVESTIGATION: CONSEQUENCES OF ABUSING ALCOHOL AND OTHER DRUGS

1. Explain that the students are to develop and act out two scenes that deal with the choice of using drugs, such as alcohol or other substances.

2. Have students suggest scenes or use the two that are shown.

ABUSING ALCOHOL
AND OTHER DRUGS
CONSEQUENCES
SCENES

Scene 1

A youngster, Rashid, has just moved to a new city and has been very sad. He is at a party and is sitting off by himself because he doesn't know anybody. Another youngster approaches Rashid and tells him that some of the people at the party are going into the kitchen to have some of the beer they found in the refrigerator. If he wants to be one of the cool people and feel a lot happier, he can join them. Rashid starts to say no, but the other youngster accuses him of being uncool, so Rashid joins them in the kitchen. He drinks two beers, and although his stomach feels a little funny, he enjoys being with the group and finds that the drinks have helped him to forget about how sad he was. Rashid continues to drink every time he is with his friends, and sometimes when he is alone. As a teenager, he remains friends with people who drink and use drugs often. He drinks more and more, gets worse and worse grades, argues often with his family, and is sick a great deal of the time.

Scene 2

Rashid is now in his thirties and is surrounded by friends, family, and coworkers as they tell him about how they know he is addicted to alcohol and how that is affecting him, his family, friends, and work. Rashid's boss tells him about how he has been doing worse and worse at work, coming in late, sleeping at work, and causing several accidents as a result of coming to work drunk. His friends tell him about how he has been losing more and more weight, getting sick more and more often, and how he has not been a friend to himself, let alone a friend to them. His wife tells him about how he has been a different person, yelling all the time, or not being there at all. His boss tells him that he will be fired unless he gets help, and his wife says that she will divorce him unless he gets help for his addiction.

3. Ask students to discuss the choices and assumptions made. Use these questions or create some of your own.

    Was this choice based on assumptions or facts?
    —assumptions

    On which assumptions was the choice based?
    —I can take as much alcohol or other drugs as I want and they won't hurt me, and I can stop when I want to.
    —I must give in to pressure to be cool and to be liked by everyone, or it would be awful.

    How could you rewrite the assumptions into provable beliefs?
    —I will be harmed by alcohol and other drugs, and eventually, I may not be able to stop when I want to.
    —I do not have to give in to pressure.

    What were the consequences of the choice?
    —drinking more and more often
    —becoming thin and ill
    —doing a poor job at school and work
    —not being a good family member or friend
    —not being a good husband

—job is threatened

—marriage is threatened

Would these consequences be acceptable to them?

—no

Was this choice based on their highest value?

—no

What might have been a better choice?

— refusing the drink and assertively sticking with this choice, trying to make friends with someone at the party who wasn't drinking, talking about their feelings regarding moving, finding things to do and ways to think that make him happy, finding non–drug-using friends

4. Have students rewrite the two scenes, using new assumptions.

REFLECTIVE
DETECTIVE

Ask students to write about the lesson in their journals.

About one week after this lesson, give students the opportunity to discuss experiences—past, present, and future—with alcohol and other drug use.

Primary Grade Modifications

No modifications needed.

Middle and High School Modifications

No modifications needed.

Sometimes, some people find themselves in unsafe situations that they have a difficult time handling on their own. First, they must try to get out of the situation themselves, as quickly as possible. If they are unable to do this alone, rather than staying in an unsafe situation, they can choose to get help from someone whom they trust.

GETTING HELP

Examples of situations for which a person may need to ask for help are situations that make one unhappy, uncomfortable, or are harmful. Figure 6.4 shows examples of times when it is important to ask for help.

ASK FOR HELP WHEN . . .

- You are very sad for a long time and you don't know why, and nothing you do helps you to feel happier.
- You are so sad or upset that you want to hurt yourself or try to end your life.
- You are not being taken care of so that you don't have enough food to eat or warm enough clothes to wear.
- You are constantly told that you are not a good person, called names, and yelled at.
- You are physically hurt by someone.
- You are being touched in places where you don't want to be touched or are being asked to touch others in places where you don't want to touch them.

Figure 6.4

In any of these situations, it is important for students to realize that they are not at fault for the situation. Also, it helps if they realize that others have experienced what they are experiencing and know how to help. It is important, as soon as they can, to find someone they trust, preferably an adult, and tell them exactly what is happening in as much detail as possible. Examples of people they might talk to would be a parent, another adult relative, an adult friend of the family, a neighbor, a teacher or another adult at school, or a trusted friend. If the first person they talk to is not able to help them leave the harmful situation, emphasize that it is important that they keep talking to people until they get the help they need and are able to leave the negative situation.

Lesson 27 examines the concept of asking for help in unsafe situations. Activity 1 has students determine specific situations in which they would get help. Activity 2 has students determine specific people they would ask to help them. Activity 3 offers rehearsal in asking for help through scene development and enactment.

You can support your students by offering to be available should they want to talk about situations in their lives. You can then access the necessary resources with which to help them.

SkyLight Training and Publishing Inc.

LESSON 27

Getting Help

TARGETED EMOTIONAL DOMAINS   Self-Awareness, Managing Emotions, Self-Control, Empathy, Handling Relationships

TARGETED INTELLIGENCES   Verbal/Linguistic, Visual/Spatial, Logical/Mathematical, Bodily/Kinesthetic, Intrapersonal, Interpersonal

CURRICULAR AREAS   Health, Social Studies, Language Arts, Math

▶ Activity 1: HELP VOTE

1. Explain that you are going to describe a variety of situations.

2. Tell students that, after you describe each situation, they are to raise their hand if they believe they would ask for help in that situation. Examples of situations that you might use include

    —Your parent hits you every day and leaves bruises on your body.

    —Your parent yells at you for making a mess in the kitchen.

    —You have been very sad all week and don't understand why, and have been thinking a lot about what it might be like to die.

    —You are sad because you have just moved to a new city.

    —Your next door neighbor asks you to touch him or her in a place where you do not want to touch him or her.

3. Give students Getting Help (see Blacklines) to add to their personal journals. Have students come up with other situations of their own. Have them discuss the kinds of situations in which they would ask for help and from whom. Also discuss the things that get in the way of asking for help such as fear and shame, and how to overcome them.

▶ Activity 2: BRAINSTORM

Tell students that they are going to brainstorm as many people as they can think of from whom they would be able to ask for help. Examples of people that students might ask for help include uncle, principal, and big brother. Ask them to write these in their journals.

▶ Activity 3: SCENE INVESTIGATION: ASKING FOR HELP

Have the students enact a scene where they are asking for help to get out of a negative situation. Ask them to decide on the situation, to choose the person from whom they are requesting help, and to describe the situation in as much detail as possible. You may play the role of the adult helper, assuring the youngster that help will be available to get out of the situation. An example scene outline is shown below for your reference. You are encouraged to solicit scene ideas from students.

ASKING FOR HELP
SCENE

Scene Idea

A youngster, Teresa, is talking to her mother. She tells her mother that when her uncle was at their house and they were alone in the den, he asked her if she would touch him in a place she did not want to touch him. When Teresa said that she didn't want to touch him there, he told her that she should be a good little niece and do what her uncle asked her to do. She left the room, feeling frightened and uncomfortable. Mother responds by assuring her daughter that she will protect her and make sure that this never happens again. She commends her for doing the right thing and coming to her for help.

Ask students to think about the scene and write a personal promise about finding help in their journals.

REFLECTIVE
DETECTIVE

Some time after this lesson, give students the opportunity to discuss past and present experiences with seeking and receiving help. Offer privacy and confidentiality for personal disclosures according to the applicable school policy.

Primary Grade Modifications

No modifications needed.

Middle and High School Modifications

HELP VOTE—Skip for this exercise.

BRAINSTORM—Skip for this exercise.

SCENE INVESTIGATION—Change the scene to consider a girl talking to her friend about her problems and her hopelessness in changing them. The friend takes her to the school counselor for help.

TAKING RISKS AND SETTING GOALS

As discussed in the very first lesson, every choice made in the present creates a chain reaction. Therefore, the choices made now determine the choices that one will be able to make in the future. (See Figure 6.5 for an overview of this discussion.)

RISK TAKING AND GOAL SETTING

Avoid Harmful Risks

- Choices not based on your beliefs but based on others' beliefs.
- Choices that are not based on your highest values.
- Choices that will make you uncomfortable or unhappy.
- Choices that will be followed by immediate or future negative consequences.
- Choices that will hurt you or others emotionally or physically.

Take Safe Risks

- Try positive, new choices about thinking.
- Try positive, new choices about feeling.
- Try positive, new choices about behaving.

Figure 6.5

People can choose to make their present choices with their futures in mind. In this way, they can choose the kind of person they want to become and use their choice-making know-how to help them choose actions that will lead toward this goal. Rather than make choices just because everyone else makes those choices or let their choices just happen, people can take the future into their hands by shaping it with every choice that they make.

In order to reach their goals, most people have to work hard, make sacrifices, and take risks. It is helpful to understand which risks are safe, which will not hurt, and which will help to achieve one's goals. People can then look at ways to help avoid unsafe risks and take safe risks, despite their fears and their tendency to want to retain their old, comfortable ways of feeling, thinking, and behaving.

Examples of unsafe risks are taking actions that may hurt one or others physically and that make one very uncomfortable or unhappy, either immediately or with future negative consequences, or actions that one believes are wrong or not truly based on one's own values. An example of an unsafe risk would be trying beer at a party.

Examples of safe risks would be taking actions based on new choices that will not hurt one or others, would make one happier, and are based on one's own beliefs. An example of a safe risk would be trying to negotiate to resolve a conflict rather than making an old choice of yelling and getting angry.

Lesson 28 helps students become part of the process of determining the kind of people they would like to be and focuses on the concepts of risk taking and goal setting. Activity 1 gives students opportunities to consider a particular risk and whether they would consider it safe or unsafe to take it. Activity 2 builds students' awareness of their own risk-taking and goal-setting behavior. Activity 3 gives students the opportunity to choose for themselves goals and behaviors that they would want as part of their characters.

Taking Risks and Setting Goals

LESSON 28

TARGETED EMOTIONAL DOMAINS Self-Awareness, Managing Emotions, Self-Control, Empathy, Handling Relationships

TARGETED INTELLIGENCES Verbal/Linguistic, Visual/Spatial, Logical/Mathematical, Bodily/Kinesthetic, Intrapersonal, Interpersonal

CURRICULAR AREAS Health, Social Studies, Language Arts, Math

▶ Activity 1: RISK VOTE

1. Explain that you are going to describe a variety of risks. Define *taking a risk* as doing something without knowing exactly what will happen.

2. After each risk, you say *safe* and *unsafe*. If the students believe that the risk would be safe to take, they are to raise their hand after you say *safe*. If they believe the risk would be unsafe to take, they raise their hand after you say *unsafe*. Examples of risks include

      —looking at someone else's test paper during a test

      —jumping off a moving train

      —acting assertively even though you are more comfortable being passive

      —taking a candy bar from a store without paying for it

—changing your self-talk so that you begin to believe that you do not have to be perfect, even though you always thought you did

—taking some time away from watching television to do homework at a regular time

—saying no to a boyfriend or girlfriend who wants you to do something you do not want to do

▶ Activity 2: GOAL SETTING

1. Prepare the Goal Setting and Risking Taking Check form by using the two column format (see Blacklines). Write the title at the top of the page. Label columns *Day* and *Actions*. Add directions: "Fill in the day and describe two actions you took to begin reaching your goal."

2. Give the Goal Setting and Risking Taking Check form to students and ask them to fill it out during the week.

▶ Activity 3: DESIGN CONTRACT

1. Explain to students that you are going to trace each of their bodies on a large piece of paper (or have pairs of students trace each other) and that each of them will prepare a contract called "The Person I Want to Be." (Give each person a large piece of paper for the outline and the contract from the Blacklines section.) On this contract, there are several areas for them to fill out. Completing these areas will help them to design the person they would like to be in the future.

2. The first area to be filled out on the contract is called "How I Choose to Feel, Think, and Act" and asks them to describe the ways in which they would like to feel, think, and act. The second area, labeled "Assumptions I Want to Change," asks them to describe assumptions they would have to change in order to feel, think, and act in the ways they have described. The third area, called "Risks and New Skills," asks them to describe risks they will take and new skills they will use in order to act in new ways. The final area, "My First Two Steps" asks them to describe the first two actions they will take immediately to begin reaching their goals. Examples of answers in these areas include

How I Choose to Feel, Think, and Act—less anxious, happier when I choose to be happy, positive self-talk, use negotiation instead of yelling, studying instead of cheating

Assumptions I Want to Change—I must be perfect; If something seems fearsome, I must get terribly upset.

Risks and New Skills—use listening skills, assertive statements

My First Two Steps—I will listen to my sister and give her feedback about what she says to me; I will spend a half hour doing homework tonight

3. After they each complete their contracts, ask them to share them with a friend or with the class. Then connect each of their contracts to their body outlines and display them on classroom walls.

About a week after this lesson, ask students to share in pairs how they are doing on their contracts, with attention to the parts they are having trouble with.

REFLECTIVE
DETECTIVE

Primary Grade Modifications

DESIGN CONTRACT—Go around the room and ask each student to briefly explain what he or she knows about each area or how he or she has changed or plans to change in each area. Fill out one contract for the class, listing several of the students' responses. Make one copy of the class contract for each student. Have each student sign or put some mark on his or her own copy, to define it personally. Then connect the individual contracts to the outlines and display them.

Middle and High School Modifications

RISK VOTE—Instead of the vote, have your students develop a list of safe risks and a list of unsafe risks. Discuss the allure of risk-taking behaviors for adolescents and some ways to address this.

DESIGN CONTRACT—Have students decide upon a way to share or display their contracts.

BLACKLINES

CONTENTS

SkyLight Training and Publishing Inc.

Title:

Directions:

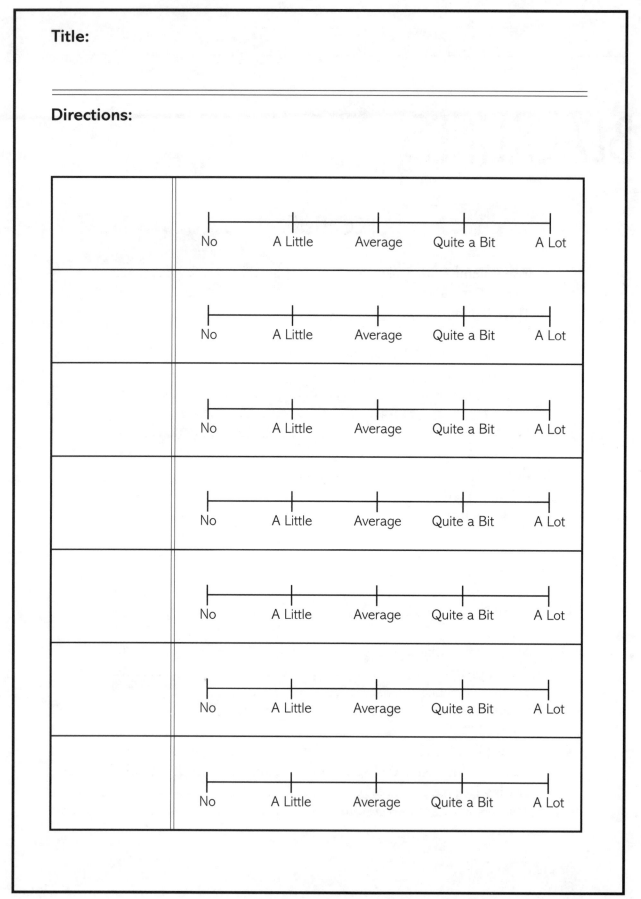

Title:

Directions:

Title:

Directions:

Title:

Directions:

The Cooperation Rules We Choose by Majority

Anxiety

INQUIRY   *I am anxious when*

ASSUMPTION

If something seems fearsome, I must get terribly upset.

Investigating Procedures

☑ Rewrite assumption into a provable belief

☑ Change thoughts

☑ Change behaviors

PROVABLE BELIEF

If something seems fearsome, I do not have to get terribly upset.

SELF-TALK

Statements I make to myself that make me feel relaxed:

Statements I make to myself that make me feel stressed:

Relax your body!

Uncovering Feelings

INQUIRY *A time when I kept my feelings inside was*

_____

_____

_____

_____

ASSUMPTION

I must never let out my feelings or it would be awful.

Investigating Procedures

- ☑ Rewrite assumption into a provable belief
- ☑ Change thoughts
- ☑ Change behaviors

PROVABLE BELIEF

I can let out my feelings.

SELF-TALK

Statements I make to myself that influence me to want to cover my feelings:	Statements I make to myself that influence me to want to uncover my feelings:

Talk about your feelings!

SkyLight Training and Publishing Inc.

Anger

A time I got angry was

_____

_____

_____

_____

ASSUMPTION

> It is awful and I must get angry when things
> don't go the way I want them to go.

Investigating Procedures

☑ Rewrite assumption into a provable belief

☑ Change thoughts

☑ Change behaviors

PROVABLE BELIEF

> Sometimes I would prefer
> things to be different than they
> are, but I do not have to get
> angry if they are not.

SELF-TALK

Statements I make to myself that influence me to get angry:	Statements I make to myself that influence me to want to seek solutions:

Look for a positive solution!

Responsibility

INQUIRY　*A time I felt totally responsible or not responsible was*

_____

_____

_____

_____

ASSUMPTION

I am responsible for everything.
I am responsible for nothing.

Investigating Procedures

☑ Rewrite assumption into a provable belief

☑ Change thoughts

☑ Change behaviors

PROVABLE BELIEF

There are certain things for which I am responsible and certain things for which I am not responsible.

SELF-TALK

Statements I make to myself that influence me to feel that I am responsible:	Statements I make to myself that influence me to feel that I am *not* responsible:

Examine the facts!

Happiness

INQUIRY *A time when I felt unhappy was*

_____
_____
_____
_____

ASSUMPTION

I can never be happy, and life will be awful unless certain things are a certain way.

Investigating Procedures

☑ Rewrite assumption into a provable belief

☑ Change thoughts

☑ Change behaviors

PROVABLE BELIEF

I can be happy if I choose to be happy.

SELF-TALK

Statements I make to myself that influence me to feel unhappy:	Statements I make to myself that influence me to feel happy:

Think about what makes you happy!

SkyLight Training and Publishing Inc.

Self-Acceptance

Accepting Ourselves

❏ I choose whether to accept myself because I am me.

❏ I choose to believe negative or positive statements others tell me and I tell myself.

❏ I can choose to tell myself positive statements.

Positive Statements: Fill in these statements.

Something I like about myself is

_____

_____

_____

I'm really good at

_____

_____

_____

I choose to accept myself because

_____

_____

_____

Self-Measurement

INQUIRY   *I sometimes feel bad about myself because, compared to everyone else, I*

_____

_____

_____

ASSUMPTION

It is awful and I must not accept myself unless
I measure up to everyone else.

 **Investigating
Procedures**

☑ Rewrite assumption
    into a provable belief

☑ Change thoughts

☑ Change behaviors

PROVABLE BELIEF

I can accept myself without
having to measure
up to anyone else.

SELF-TALK

Statements I make to myself
that influence me to measure
myself against others:

Statements I make to myself
that influence me to accept
myself:

Set realistic goals for yourself!

Perfectionism

INQUIRY *A time I felt that I had to be perfect was*

_____

_____

_____

_____

ASSUMPTION

If I am not always perfect, it is awful.

Investigating Procedures

☑ Rewrite assumption into a provable belief

☑ Change thoughts

☑ Change behaviors

PROVABLE BELIEF

I do not have to be perfect.

SELF-TALK

Statements I make to myself that influence me to want to be perfect:	Statements I make to myself that influence me to want to learn from mistakes:

Enjoy learning from your mistakes!

SkyLight Training and Publishing Inc.

Friendship

INQUIRY *One way that I now act with my friends is that I*

_____

_____

_____

_____

ASSUMPTION

I will never be able to do anything to be a better friend.

Investigating Procedures

☑ Rewrite assumption into a provable belief

☑ Change thoughts

☑ Change behaviors

PROVABLE BELIEF

There are some things I can do to be a better friend.

SELF-TALK

Statements I make to myself that influence me to want to make negative friendship choices:

Statements I make to myself that influence me to want to make positive friendship choices:

Try better friendship choices!

Family

INQUIRY   *One way that I now act with my family is that I*

_____

_____

_____

_____

ASSUMPTION

I will never be able to do anything to be a better family member.

Investigating Procedures

☑ Rewrite assumption into a provable belief

☑ Change thoughts

☑ Change behaviors

PROVABLE BELIEF

There are some things I can do to be a better family member.

SELF-TALK

Statements I make to myself that influence me to make negative family choices:

Statements I make to myself that influence me to make positive family choices:

Try better family choices!

Put-Downs

INQUIRY   *A put-down I once said to someone was*

_____
_____
_____
_____

ASSUMPTION

In order to feel good about myself, I must try to make someone else feel bad about him- or herself.

Investigating Procedures

☑ Rewrite assumption into a provable belief

☑ Change thoughts

☑ Change behaviors

PROVABLE BELIEF

I don't have to try to make others feel bad about themselves in order to feel good about myself.

SELF-TALK

Statements I make to myself that influence me to put down others:

Statements I make to myself that influence me to build up others:

Help others to feel good!

SkyLight Training and Publishing Inc.

Pressuring

INQUIRY *A time I pressured someone was when*

_____

_____

_____

_____

ASSUMPTION

I must pressure others in order to always
have my way, or it will be awful.

Investigating Procedures

☑ Rewrite assumption
   into a provable belief

☑ Change thoughts

☑ Change behaviors

PROVABLE BELIEF

I do not have to pressure
others to have my way.

SELF-TALK

Statements I make to myself
that influence me to pressure
others:

Statements I make to myself
that influence me to directly ask
for what I want:

Ask for what you want!

SkyLight Training and Publishing Inc.

Being Pressured

INQUIRY *A time I gave in to pressure was*

_____

_____

_____

_____

ASSUMPTION

I must give in to pressure to be cool and to be
liked by everyone, or it will be awful.

Investigating Procedures

☑ Rewrite assumption
into a provable belief

☑ Change thoughts

☑ Change behaviors

PROVABLE BELIEF

I do not have to give
in to pressure to be cool and
to be liked by everyone.

SELF-TALK

Statements I make to myself
that influence me to give in to
pressure:

Statements I make to myself
that influence me to take pride
in my own choices:

Take pride in your choices!

Prejudice

INQUIRY *A time I believed I was better than someone else was*

_____

_____

_____

_____

ASSUMPTION

If someone is different than me, he or she is
not as good a person as I am.

**Investigating
Procedures**

☑ Rewrite assumption
into a provable belief

☑ Change thoughts

☑ Change behaviors

PROVABLE BELIEF

If someone is different than
me, they are just
as good a person as I am.

SELF-TALK

Statements I make to myself
that influence me to be preju-
diced toward others:

Statements I make to myself
that influence me to be accepting of others:

Look at the whole person!

Manipulation Check

Fill in the day, then put a check mark in the appropriate box depending on how you tried to get what you wanted that day.

DAY	Whine	Act Out	Command	Threaten	Accuse	Label	Ask Directly

Asking Directly

❏ "I'd like it if you would pay more attention to me."

❏ "Could I have some of your candy?"

❏ "I would really like a lick of your ice cream."

Assertive Statements: Please complete the following sentences with a statement that asks directly for what you want.

If the teacher is paying attention to other students and doesn't see that I want attention, I could say:

_____

_____

_____

_____

If my friend has a new game that I want to play, I could say:

_____

_____

_____

_____

Feedback Practice

Jim is going to tell you about something that happened to him yesterday. After you read the story, check off the sentence that you believe would be feedback based on just the hard facts of what he said.

"In school yesterday, the teacher announced that we were going to have a test. When she said that, I realized that I could have gotten nervous about it, and my stomach might have started hurting. Instead, I took deep breaths and told myself that I would probably do well on the test. I told myself that the worst thing that could happen would be that I might have to take the test again, and that wouldn't be so awful. I took the test and got 100."

❑ "You got smart and stopped being chicken about the test."

❑ "You talked to yourself and took deep breaths and did well on the test."

❑ "You should have done the rag exercise also."

Assertiveness

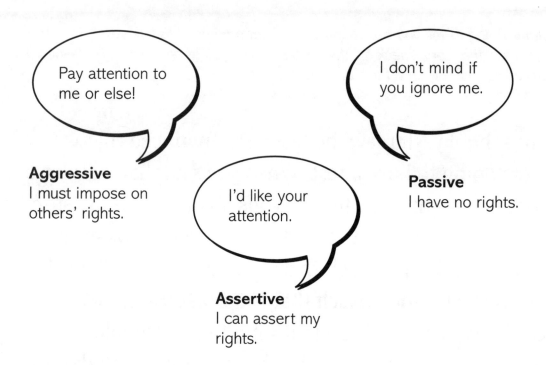

Aggressive
I must impose on others' rights.

Assertive
I can assert my rights.

Passive
I have no rights.

Assertive Statements: Please complete the following sentences with a statement that asserts your rights without imposing on anyone else's rights.

If somebody took something that belonged to me, I could say:

_____
_____
_____
_____

If I wanted to have a lick of my friend's ice cream cone, I could ask:

_____
_____
_____
_____

Study Skills

PROVABLE BELIEF

I can achieve success in school!

A STUDY SKILL FOR ME

Please complete the following sentence.

One skill that could help me do better in school is

_____
_____

_____
_____
_____
_____

Study Skills

- ☑ Organize desk and materials.
- ☑ Follow directions.
- ☑ Make an outline.
- ☑ Write a summary.
- ☑ Do homework . . .
  in a special place
  at a special time
  give yourself a reward.

SELF-TALK

Statements I make to myself that influence me to feel I can be successful:

Study Skills Check

Fill in the day, and check off the study skill you practiced that day.

DAY	Organized	Directions	Outline	Summary	Homework

SkyLight Training and Publishing Inc.

Clarifying Values and Consequences

Consequences: what happens as a result of our choices.

Draw a line between the choice and the consequence that might result because of that choice. An example has been provided.

Cheating one time ○	○ Going to jail
Stealing money ○	○ Liking yourself less and less
Taking a drink of alcohol ○	○ Worrying about success without cheating
Putting yourself down ○	○ Family getting along well
Trying to listen to family members ○	○ Drinking more and more alcohol
Choosing without thinking ○	○ Having lots of friends
Being friendly to others ○	○ Making poor choices

Getting Help

Ask for Help When . . .

✓ You are very sad for a long time and don't know why, and nothing you do helps you feel happier.

✓ You are so sad or upset that you want to hurt yourself or try to end your life.

✓ You are not being taken care of so that you don't have enough food to eat or warm enough clothes to wear.

✓ You are constantly being told that you are not a good person, being called names, and being yelled at.

✓ You are physically hurt by someone.

✓ You are being touched by others in places where you don't want to be touched or are being asked by others to touch them in places where you don't want to touch them.

Get out of the situation if you can.

Find an adult you trust and tell him or her exactly what happened.

Adults you can ask for help include a(n):

❑ Parent or guardian
❑ Aunt or uncle
❑ Adult friend of the family
❑ Neighbor
❑ Teacher
❑ Principal

The Person I Want to Be Contract

How I Choose to Feel, Think, and Act

Assumptions I Want to Change

Risks and New Skills

My First Two Steps

SkyLight Training and Publishing Inc.

SUMMARY ACTIVITIES

The first two summary activities in this appendix are keyed to the first two parts of *Teaching for Intelligence*. The third summary activity covers all the lessons in the book. These summary activities pull together the lessons and provide an opportunity for students to summarize and revisit the different choice-making skills and competencies that they worked on in the activities.

Choosing to Feel Positive

INDIVIDUAL ACTIVITY

Ask students to complete these sentences in their journals:

— When it comes to anxiety, now I . . .

— When it comes to uncovering feelings, now I . . .

— When it comes to anger, now I . . .

— When it comes to responsibility, now I . . .

— When it comes to happiness, now I . . .

SUMMARY ACTIVITY FOR PART I

GROUP ACTIVITY

1. Announce that students are to do group projects. Each project covers one of the five assumptions that were important to developing emotional intelligence through self-awareness and managing emotions.

2. Divide the class into five groups. Assign one of the five assumptions in the unit to each group:

    Anxiety: If something seems fearsome, I must get terribly upset.

    Feelings: I must never let my feelings out or it would be awful.

    Anger: It is awful and I must get angry when things do not go they way I want them to go.

    Responsibility: I am responsible for everything. I am responsible for nothing.

    Happiness: I can never be happy, and life will be awful unless certain things are a certain way.

3. Each group is responsible for developing their assigned project, based on the assumption they have been given. The project may be a scene to be acted out; a poem or story to be read; a drawing to be described and displayed; a song, dance, or scientific experiment; or any other form that they choose.

4. Their project centers on a famous person of their choice who, at first, believes in the assumption they are treating. They will share this person's thoughts, feelings, and behaviors as a result of believing in the assumption. Their famous person discovers clues that help him or her to change the assumption to a provable belief. They let us know how the clues were discovered and how they were used. They also let us know the person's new thoughts, feelings, and behaviors as a result of believing in the new, provable belief.

5. Each group shares their project with the rest of the class. This can take any form the project demands. They may choose to videotape these and play them back at a later date.

Primary Grade Modifications

INDIVIDUAL ACTIVITY—Ask students the questions aloud, summarize the responses of the class on a sheet of paper, and give copies to the students.

GROUP ACTIVITY—Have each student create a drawing, painting, or collage to reflect each of the five assumptions. Hang each student's art, and have him or her describe the work in a "gallery tour."

Middle and High School Modifications

No modifications needed.

Choosing to Think Wisely

INDIVIDUAL ACTIVITY

Ask students to complete these sentences in their journals:

      —When it comes to self-acceptance, now I . . .

      —When it comes to self-measurement, now I . . .

      —When it comes to perfectionism, now I . . .

      —When it comes to friendship, now I . . .

      —When it comes to family, now I . . .

      —When it comes to put-downs, now I . . .

      —When it comes to pressuring peers, now I . . .

      —When it comes to being pressured, now I . . .

      —When it comes to being prejudiced, now I . . .

GROUP ACTIVITY

1. Students do a group project that covers the emotional competencies developed through discovering self-concept, relationships, and empathy experiences.

2. Divide the class into seven groups. Assign one of the following concepts to each group—self-measurement, perfectionism, friendship, family, put-downs, peer pressure, and prejudice.

3. Each group is responsible for writing and illustrating an entry for a book about positive choices. Each group's entry talks about the best possible choices to make with regard to their concept. The entry can be in any form. Some examples might be a letter to and response from Dear Abby, a recipe of how to make a good choice in that area, a step-by-step list of directions, a "chemical" formula, a mathematical equation, "ten commandments" of making the choice, a poem, or a story.

4. Remind students that their entry covers the provable belief associated with their concept, and deals with thoughts, feelings, and behaviors.

5. Have the students read their entries aloud.

Primary Grade Modifications

INDIVIDUAL ACTIVITY—Ask students the questions aloud, summarize the responses of the class on a sheet of paper, and give copies to the students.

SkyLight Training and Publishing Inc.

GROUP ACTIVITY—Have each group create a drawing, painting, or collage to reflect each of the seven assumptions. Hang each group's art, and have one group member describe the work in a "gallery tour."

—If you choose, lead the class in a group project for each assumption, such as a simple song or movement piece or a brief role-play. Consider videotaping and playing the results of the full class project.

Middle and High School Modifications

GROUP ACTIVITY—Give students the choice to use media other than writing. Additional project options can include a piece created on computer, a video, a class lesson, a song, or a dance.

SUMMARY ACTIVITY FOR PART III

Choosing to Act Sensibly

This is a summary for all the choice-making lessons.

INDIVIDUAL ACTIVITY

Ask students to complete the following sentences in their journals:

> —The person I want to be:
>
> —New ways I want to think:
>
> —New ways I want to feel:
>
> —New ways I want to behave:
>
> —Assumptions I want to change:
>
> —Safe risks I will take:
>
> —Skills I will use:
>
> —Two actions I will take immediately:

GROUP ACTIVITY

1. Form small groups of five or six students.

2. Ask each group to develop a story that portrays what the group members have learned from the choice-making lessons, using their personal handouts and their journals. One possible story structure is a class reunion fifteen years in

the future where students gather to talk about the choices they have made that have led them to their goals. Or students might create a fairy tale that describes a world based on assumptions, where many negative choices were made, that somehow developed into a world based on beliefs, where positive choices are made. Students are encouraged to create their own story structures.

3. After creating the story, each group develops and presents it as a short scene. Each student is to take some part in this dramatization. Remind them of the steps involved in preparing a scene. They may present the scene in whatever form they choose: taped, sung, danced, drawn, performed, painted, and so on.

Whichever form the project takes, sharing reinforces for students what they have developed with others. This allows students to make a statement about the positive choices they want to make and be rewarded for doing so. Rather than focusing on the quality of the format of the story, focus on content. This reinforces lessons taught and encourages your students to take responsibility for new choices.

4. Each group presents its scene to the class, another class, their parents, the school, or some other suitable audience.

Primary Grade Modifications

INDIVIDUAL ACTIVITY—Ask students the questions aloud, summarize the responses of the class on a sheet of paper, and give copies to the students.

Middle and High School Modifications

No modifications needed.

REFERENCES

Burke, K. 1992. *What to do with the kid who: Developing cooperation, self-discipline, and responsibility in the classroom.* Palatine, Ill.: IRI/Skylight Publishing.

Chapman, C. 1993. *If the shoe fits: How to develop multiple intelligences in the classroom.* Palatine, Ill.: IRI/Skylight Publishing.

Cowan, M. M., and F. M. Clover. 1991. Enhancement of self-concept through discipline-based art education. *Art Education* 44: 41–49.

Deline, J. 1991. Why can't they get along? *Journal of Physical Education, Recreation, and Dance* 62: 21–28.

Dewhurst, D. W. 1991. Should teachers enhance their pupils' self-esteem? *Journal of Moral Education* 20: 10–15.

Ellis, A. 1990. *How to stubbornly refuse to make yourself miserable about anything, yes, anything.* New York: First Carol.

Erin, J. N., K. Dignan, and P. A. Brown. 1991. Are social skills teachable? A review of the literature. *Journal of Visual Impairment and Blindness* 85: 60–72.

Gardner, H. 1983. *Frames of mind.* New York: Bantam Books.

Gibson, R. L. 1989. Prevention and the elementary school counselor. *Elementary School Guidance and Counseling* 24: 30–37.

Goleman, D. 1995. *Emotional intelligence.* New York: Bantam Books.

Jones, R. M., K. Kline, S. A. Habkirk, and A. Saler. 1990. Teacher characteristics and competencies related to substance abuse prevention. *Journal of Drug Education* 20: 182–198.

Mayer, M. 1990. The play's the thing. *Momentum* 15: 65–72.

Meyer, J. R. 1990. Democratic values and their development. *Social Studies* 81: 199–206.

Rolan, A. J. 1991. Personal and social education: Citizenship and biography. *Journal of Moral Education* 20: 27–36.

Rotheram, M. J. 1982. Social skills training with underachievers, disruptive and exceptional children. *Psychology in the Schools* 19: 532–539.

INDEX

SkyLight Training and Publishing Inc.

There are
one-story intellects,
two-story intellects, and
three-story intellects with skylights.

All fact collectors, who have no aim beyond their facts, are

one-story minds.

Two-story minds
compare, reason, generalize,
using the labors of the fact collectors
as well as their own.

Three-story minds
idealize, imagine, predict—their best illumination
comes from above,

through the **skylight**.

—Oliver Wendell Holmes

SkyLight
Professional
Development

PROFESSIONAL DEVELOPMENT

We Prepare Your Teachers Today
for the Classrooms of Tomorrow

Learn from Our Books and from Our Authors!

Ignite Learning in Your School or District.

SkyLight's team of classroom-experienced consultants can help you foster systemic change for increased student achievement.

Professional development is a process not an event. SkyLight's experienced practitioners drive the creation of our on-site professional development programs, graduate courses, research-based publications, interactive video courses, teacher-friendly training materials, and online resources—call SkyLight Professional Development today.

SkyLight specializes in three professional development areas.

Specialty #  **Best Practices**

We **model** the best practices that result in improved student performance and guided applications.

Specialty #  **Making the Innovations Last**

We help set up **support** systems that make innovations part of everyday practice in the long-term systemic improvement of your school or district.

Specialty #  **How to Assess the Results**

We prepare your school leaders to encourage and **assess** teacher growth, **measure** student achievement, and **evaluate** program success.

Contact the SkyLight team and begin a process toward long-term results.

2626 S. Clearbrook Dr., Arlington Heights, IL 60005
800-348-4474 • 847-290-6600 • FAX 847-290-6609
info@skylightedu.com • www.skylightedu.com